A DEVOTIONAL JOURNAL

GREATER WORKS:
MIRACLES
SIGNS
AND
WONDERS

DR. DORAL R. PULLEY

**Greater Works:
Miracles Signs and Wonders**

ISBN: 9798876846679

Copyright © 2024 COTEK Press, Dr. Doral R. Pulley

All rights reserved.

No part of this book may be reproduced in any form without the permission or expressed consent from its author and/or publisher.

ACKNOWLEDGMENTS

I thank God for Executive Cord of the Church of the Everlasting, Kingdom. It is my distinct pleasure to be a part of a three-fold cord with great men of God such as Bishop A. Bernard Hector, Vice Presiding Prelate and Bishop D. Walter Rogers, Jr., our Vicar General.

I appreciate Overseer Julius L. Ford, General Secretary of the Church of the Everlasting Kingdom, Inc. for designing the cover for this book. We have an incredible synergy that makes projects a joy to complete. These endeavors not only bless us, but they expand the Kingdom.

My heart is full of gratitude for the Presidium, Spiritual Leaders, Five-Fold Leaders, and Ecclesiastical Leaders of the Church of the Everlasting Kingdom. Thanks for sharing your testimonies about Miracles, Signs, and Wonders.

I AM grateful for Minister Gina L. Folk for partnering with me in preaching and teaching this series with me on the Miracles, Signs, and Wonders of Jesus Christ. Your tenacity ensure that every account was covered with life application.

I celebrate my spiritual son. Brother David Pulley, for organizing this message series in such a way that it was easy for me to write and develop the ideas.

I thank God for Minister Mother Linda Johnson for your flexibility and patience with me in editing.

My heart is full gratitude for my spiritual daughter, Elder Keesha Howard, for pushing me to explain in grave detail the greater works.

I appreciate Brother Vernon for being a major support system. When I needed encouragement, I was able to look to you.

FOREWORD

Miracles, Signs & Wonders

"This is the LORD'S doing; it is marvelous in our eyes."
Psalm 118:23, KSB

I have been graced, gifted and blessed to operate in the Office of the Prophet for some time now. I have seen God do tremendous things not only in my own life, but in the life of others as well.

"And this will be a sign to you…"
Luke 2:12, KSB

Throughout my lifetime, I have experienced and continue to experience what I refer to as *indicators*. Typically, these *indicators* are subtle suggestions that something or some instance or occurrence is not a mere coincidence or happenstance. In Kingdom, we know that NOTHING JUST HAPPENS. These *indicators* serve as signs from God to allow us advance knowledge and perspective for something upcoming. In Daniel 5:5, it was referred to as the "handwriting on the wall."

The signs of God serve as a support system for the life of a believer. When we know God, and have relationship with God, we speak God's language, we recognize God's "body language" and understand when God desires to reveal or show us something in advance.

"You have eyes, do you not see? You have ears, do you not hear? Do you not remember?"
Mark 8:18, KSB

As we continue in our journeys of consciousness, may we be always alert, mindful and observant of the signs and wonders of God in order to behold each and every manifesting miracle around us. Amen

Bishop A. Bernard Hector
Kingdom Covenant Ministries, Spiritual Leader
Baltimore, MD
COTEK, Vice Presiding Prelate

Table of Contents

Week 1 – Overview 10
Day 1 – Biblical Fasting 10
Day 2 – The 40 Day Experience 13
Day 3 – Consecration 15
Day 4 – I AM a Miracle! 18
Day 5 – I AM the Sign! 19
Day 6 – I AM a Wonder! 20
Day 7 – No Discrimination 21

Week 2 – Miracles of the Head and Face 25
Day 8 – All the way! 25
Day 9 – Give me back my ear! 27
Day 10 – It's about the glory! 28
Day 11 – Asked and Answered! 30
Day 12 – Let's Do It Again! 31
Day 13 – The Journey to Openness 33
Day 14 – It's About Time! 35

Week 3 – Diverse Miracles 40
Day 15 – This is how we do it! 40
Day 16 – You Give Me Fever! 42
Day 17 – Through the Roof! 43
Day 18 – How to Make the Swelling Go Down! 45
Day 19 – Healing Vocabulary 46
Day 20 – The Heritage to Heal and be a Healer 48
Day 21 – Impregnated with Purpose 50

Week 4 – Healing Lengthy Illnesses and Contagious Diseases 51
Day 22 – What kind of party are you having? 51
Day 23 – I Heal Myself! 53
Day 24 – Love Lifted Me! 55
Day 25 – What is it going to take for you to Straighten Up? ... 57

Day 26 – From Healing to Wholeness 59
Day 27 – Not Too Late for a Miracle 60
Day 28 – A Change of HAART 62

Week 5 – Exorcisms & Resurrections 64
Day 29 – Casting out your demons! 64
Day 30 – Oink, Oink 66
Day 31 – Home Alone 68
Day 32 – Church devils 70
Day 33 – The Mighty I AM Power! 72
Day 34 – Essential Personnel Only! 73
Day 35 – Cancel the Contradiction! 76

Week 6 – Signs and Wonders 78
Day 36 – Look What We Can Do! 79
Day 37 – Live Your Best Life! 81
Day 38 – Moving Mountains 85
Day 39 – The Great Awakening 87
Day 40 – One last fish sandwich 88
Day 41 – Show me the money! 90
Day 42 – The Lifestyle of a Water Walker 91

Week 7 – These Works and Greater Works 95
Day 43 – More Time to Do Greater Works 95
Day 44 – Greater Works – More Housing 97
Day 45 – Greater Works – More Healing Places 98
Day 46 – Greater Works – More Freedom 99
Day 47 – Greater Works – More People 100
Day 48 – Greater Works – More Leaders, Assemblies, Ministries, and Businesses 102
Day 49 – Greater Works – More Writing 103

Unveiling of the Seal 106
Seal of the International Evangelist of COTEK 106

Week 1 – Overview

Day 1 – Biblical Fasting
Day 2 – Feasting
Day 3 – Consecration
Day 4 – I AM a Sign!
Day 5 – I AM a Wonder!
Day 6 – I AM a Miracle!
Day 7 – No discrimination in Miracles, Signs, and Wonders

Day 1 – Biblical Fasting

Read – Isaiah 58:1-15

> *"They ask, 'Why have we fasted, and you have not seen it? Why have we humbled ourselves, and you have not noticed (Isaiah 58:3)?"* KSB

Fasting and forgiving is a powerful prayer tool that helps us to live holistically healthy, balanced, and well-rounded lives. Biblical leaders modeled fasting for us. Jesus, our Wayshower, fasted and taught his disciples to fast as well (Matthew 6:16-18). Paul, an apostle of Jesus Christ, also reinforced the principles of fasting in his epistles to the local assemblies. He told them that he fasted often (II Corinthians 11:27)."

There are diverse types of fasts in the Bible. One type of fast is the absolute fast. In the absolute fast, people such as Moses (Exodus 34:28-34) and Jesus (Luke 4:1-13) were set apart for 40 days without food or water. Other fasts were for shorter periods of time. Esther and her maidens fasted for three days and three nights (Esther 4:1-5:5). Also, Jonah did a three day and three nights fast in the belly of the great fish (Jonah 3:1-10). Other fasts called for people to abstain from certain foods and drinks for an extended period as Daniel and the three Hebrew boys did (Daniel 10:1-21). The fast in this devotional resembles Daniel's fast.

Consecration 2024 **Fasting Options**

"For as many as are led by the Spirit, they are the offspring of the Spirit (Romans 8:14)."

Progressive	Weekly	Daniel (Focus on Items)	Intermittent (Focus on Hours)	Fasting & Feasting
Increase your daily water intake to 64 ounces or more	Increase your daily water intake to 64 ounces or more	No meats and no sweets	12 Hours *(6 am – 6 pm)* 16 hours *(12 am – 4 pm)* 18 hours *(12 am – 6 pm)* 20 hours *(8 pm – 4 pm)*	Fasting from secular music and feasting on Gospel, Christian, Inspirational, and Meditative Music
8 Hours of Absolute Fasting. No eating between 8 pm – 4 am; Only water	8 Hours of Absolute Fasting No eating between 8 pm – 4 am. Only water	No meats and no sweets	12 Hours *(6 am – 6 pm)* 16 hours *(12 am – 4 pm)* 18 hours *(12 am – 6 pm)* 20 hours *(8 pm – 4 pm)*	Fasting from social media and feasting fellowship with family and friends through conversations and outings
No coffee, tea, soda, alcohol or drinks with artificial flavors or sweeteners. Drink water, teas, milk and 100% fruit juices.	No coffee, tea, soda, alcohol or drinks with artificial flavors or sweeteners. Drink water, teas, milk and 100% fruit juices.	No meats and no sweets	12 Hours *(6 am – 6 pm)* 16 hours *(12 am – 4 pm)* 18 hours *(12 am – 6 pm)* 20 hours *(8 pm – 4 pm)*	Fasting from profanity and complaining and feasting on quoting scriptures, denials, and affirmations and positive words to others
No fried foods Instead grill, bake, broil, boil or steam your foods	No fried foods Instead grill, bake, broil, boil or steam your foods	No meats and no sweets	12 Hours *(6 am – 6 pm)* 16 hours *(12 am – 4 pm)* 18 hours *(12 am – 6 pm)* 20 hours *(8 pm – 4 pm)*	Fasting from alcohol and feasting on spiritual highs through thanksgiving, praise, and worship

No desserts No sweets such as candy, cookies, cakes, donuts, pudding, pastries, ice cream,	No desserts No sweets such as candy, cookies, cakes, donuts, pudding, pastries, ice cream,	No meats and no sweets	12 Hours *(6 am – 6 pm)* 16 hours *(12 am – 4 pm)* 18 hours *(12 am – 6 pm)* 20 hours *(8 pm – 4 pm)*	Fasting from smoking and vaping and feasting on mediation, mindfulness and breathing
No pasta and no starches such as bread of any kind, potatoes, rice, pizza, etc.	No pasta and no starches such as bread of any kind, potatoes, rice, pizza, etc.	No meats and no sweets	12 Hours *(6 am – 6 pm)* 16 hours *(12 am – 4 pm)* 18 hours *(12 am – 6 pm)* 20 hours *(8 pm – 4 pm)*	Fasting from television and movies and feasting on visioning and visualization
No meat and no dairy. Consume only fruits, vegetables, 100% fruit juices, water	No meat and no dairy. Consume only fruits, vegetables, 100% fruit juices, water	No meats and no sweets	12 Hours *(6 am – 6 pm)* 16 hours *(12 am – 4 pm)* 18 hours *(12 am – 6 pm)* 20 hours *(8 pm – 4 pm)*	Fasting from unnecessary conversation and movement and feasting on stillness and silence

* If you are on medication or have any health challenges, be sure to consult with your physician and make the necessary modifications to the fast.

Day 2 – The 40 Day Experience

Read – Luke 4:1-13

"Jesus, full of the Holy Spirit, left the Jordan and was led by the Spirit into the wilderness, where he was tempted for forty days. He ate nothing during those days, and at the end of them he was very hungry (Luke 4:1-2)." KSB

Most biblical leaders had a 40-Day experience. For example, Noah was in the flood for 40 days and 40 nights (Genesis 7:12). Therefore, Noah shows us that it may take 40 days to wash out our old thoughts, speech, and behavior patterns. Goliath taunted the armies of Israel for 40 days before David defeated him with the sling shot and the smooth stones (I Samuel 17:16). David shows us that it may take 40 days of consistent negative results before we get tired of a situation and are ready to open our minds to really do something about it. Elijah, the prophet, stayed on Mt. Horeb 40 days and rested after fleeing from Jezebel (I Kings 19:8). Elijah shows us that we may need 40 days to rest and reflect before we make our next move or begin our next assignment. Ezekiel, the prophet, laid on his right side for 40 days to represent the children of Israel wandering in the wilderness for 40 years (Ezekiel 4:6). Ezekiel shows us that it may take us 40 days of demonstration before we really get the point.

Forty days was also significant in the life and ministry of Jesus. Jesus, our Wayshower, was in the wilderness for 40 days and 40 nights fasting (Matthew 4:2). Like Jesus, we are entering into a time of consecration for 40 days so that we will be empowered and equipped to do what God has called us to do. Jesus' disciples saw him for 40 days before he ascended back into heaven (Acts 1:3). It may take us 40 days for us to be able to see Jesus in a new way.

This Lenten Season Consecration is 40 days over a 7-week period. It begins on Ash Wednesday and continues through Good Friday. Taking Sundays off gives us a total of 40 days of consecration. The Sunday respite is an opportunity to prepare for the challenge of the next week. Others may choose another day during the week other than Sunday to take off due to an annual family event or a required work obligation.

Day 3 – Consecration

Read – John 16:12-15

"Those who are led by the Spirit of God demonstrate that they are the offspring of God (Romans 8:14)." KSB

Consecration is more than abstaining from certain foods or an attempt to get rid of weight. Consecration is a time to focus and consecrate on our holistic growth and development. Consecration is about being conscious of what we are eating, when we are eating, why we are eating, where we are eating, how much we are eating as well as what foods and beverages we may have become dependent on and feel that we cannot do without.

Because it is your personal consecration to the Lord, there is more than one way to do it. Some do the progressive fast where they add or delete something from their diet each week and build up to the point of only eating fruits, vegetables, water, nuts, and lentils. Others find it beneficial to do a weekly fast and only eat or delete what is suggested for that week. Some do intermittent fasting for 12, 16, or 18 hours. For others, it may be helpful to not focus on foods and beverages at all. Instead, they focus on fasting from unhealthy coping mechanisms and feasting on spiritual practices. Find more about the consecration options on pages 12 and 13.

Pray about it and ask the Holy Spirit to lead you in your decision. Also, consult with your physician. Bless and take your medications as prescribed. There is nothing wrong with inviting family, friends, coworkers, classmates, and neighbors to join you. Consider being a part of a support group or hosting a study group. Deep down everyone desires to be healthy and live a better life.

A MIRACLE PRESCRIPTION FOR PAIN

Bishop D. Walter Rogers, Jr.
Beyond Church, Spiritual Leader
Washington, DC
COTEK, Vicar General

A personal miracle is often described as an extraordinary event or experience that defies natural explanation and is a divine intervention or a sign of God's presence in someone's life. Miracles can vary significantly from one person to another and are highly subjective. What may be considered a miracle to one person might not be seen as such by another.

Many years ago, I found myself experiencing feelings of depression. There was so much happening in my life all at once, and the weight of it all seemed too much for me to bear. At that time, there appeared to be only one way to experience some type of relief from all the pain, feelings of sadness, and depression, and that was to "sleep or rest."

I found myself ingesting over seventy Excedrin Extra Strength pills; it was a pain reliever! An overdose has side effects that include liver damage, kidney damage, and intestinal bleeding, just to name a few.

Fast forward, I am rushed into the emergency room, in and out of consciousness, hooked up to machines with doctors and nurses surround me. During one of the times, I was conscious, I remember the doctor saying, "This does not look good for him; his aspirin levels are off the charts, his heart rate is dangerously high, and his kidneys are working overtime."

At this moment, I just knew that this was potentially my last moment on this earth. I began to cry because I did not desire to commit suicide; I just desired rest and relief from everything.

I closed my eyes with tears running down my face, and when I opened them, the room was empty, but there was one nurse (who I later learned was an angel) checking monitors and levels. She turned to me and said, "Baby, what are you doing? Do you know that it simply is not your time yet?" She held my hand and said just pray. I cried even more, talked to God, prayed for a miracle to happen, and said if you do this for me, I promise I will never give up on my purpose.

As I said, amen, the room was filled with nurses and doctors, standing in amazement because every level in my body was back to normal. They thought the machines had malfunctioned, ran more tests and blood work, and came out with the same result.

I desire to encourage someone that God can still perform a miracle in your life, even with self-inflicted nonsense! I AM a living witness!

Day 4 – I AM a Miracle!

Read – Matthew 13:53-58

"God anointed Jesus of Nazareth with the Holy Ghost and with power. Therefore, he went about doing good and healing all those who were under the power of the devil because God was with him (Acts 10:38)." KSB

Jesus was a miracle, a sign, and a wonder. His birth, life, ministry, death, burial, resurrection, and ascension were full of miracles, signs, and wonders. He was able to perform miracles, signs, and wonders because he realized that, he in fact, was a demonstration of God's love and a manifestation of God's power.

Biblical miracles are most often associated with healing, health, and wholeness. The more we realize that God is in us, God flows through us, and God functions as us, we will experience and perform more miracles. Two of the most powerful words that we can say are, "I AM." When we declare that I AM a miracle the blind will see, the deaf will hear, the dumb will talk, the lame will walk, people with diseases will be healed, negative influences will be cast out, and the dead will be raised.

Do you believe in miracles? Can heaven manifest on the earth? Do you believe that the impossible is possible? Can the intangible become tangible? Can the invisible become visible?

_____

_____

_____

_____

_____

Day 5 – I AM the Sign!

Read – Matthew 24:1-14

"The Jews then responded to him, "What sign can you show us to prove your authority to do all this (John 2:16)?" KSB

Miracles, signs, and wonders are often used interchangeably. The major difference between a miracle and a sign is healing. A sign is a demonstration of God's power that does not have anything to do with sickness, pain, disease, discomfort, or dysfunction in the body. Jesus, our Wayshower, performed signs every time he took something that already existed and changed it to serve more people; like turning the water into wine. Another example of a sign is when he multiplied the two fish and five loaves of bread to feed thousands.

Jesus was a sign. His mere presence gained people's attention and gave God glory. Signs get our attention and show us that God can do what appears impossible. When we realize that we are signs, we will manifest more external signs.

Signs call our attention to things and give us direction. Stop – red light, yield – yellow light, and proceed – green light. Stop the ego, yield to the Holy Spirit, and proceed to your good. The one-way sign empowers us to let go of our way and do it God's way. The dead-end sign tells us not to go that way because we have tried it before, and it is a dead-end for us. God gives us opportunities to take a detour and go in a different direction. God speaks to people through our experiences, and we become signs.

Are you open to allowing people to get their signs through your experiences and testimony?

Day 6 – I AM a Wonder!

Read – Hebrews 2:1-4

"People of Israel, hear these words; Jesus of Nazareth was a man approved by God. God performed miracles, wonders, and signs through him. You know it because he did it right in your midst (Acts 2:22)." KSB

Jesus, our Wayshower, did miracles, signs, and wonders because he recognized his divinity. Different than miracles and signs, wonders have to do with nature. Some examples of Jesus Christ demonstrating his dominion over nature are defying gravity and walking on water as well as calming the raging sea with his words, "Peace be still."

Like Jesus, we are superheroes, and we have the superpower. When we remember our divinity, and operate in the super consciousness, we manifest wonders. We must go beyond the physical limitations of this life to express as the superheroes that we are. We have the wonderworking power inside of us, it just needs to be activated. God is all power. God is our wonder power, and we activate our wonder power through our Kingdom Practices for the Development of the Soul.

Because wonders happen in nature, even amid hurricanes, tornadoes, volcanoes, fires, floods, pandemics, we know that God is working during them. Instead of seeing these events as attacks of the devil, we see them as opportunities for the earth to do its functions as a living organism. Instead of viewing these occurrences as catastrophes, tragedies, and crisis, we see them as an opportunity for us to manifest God's presence and for people to come together to support one another.

Day 7 – No Discrimination

Read – Matthew 4:23-25

"Jesus went through all the towns and villages, teaching in their synagogues, preaching the gospel of the Kingdom and healing every disease and sickness among the people (Matthew 9:35)." KSB

Jesus Christ loved everybody. He even ate with the publicans and sinners (Matthew 9:9-12). He received a lot of persecution from the religious leaders of his day because he loved and interacted with all types of people. However, Jesus did not allow their prejudices to affect his love. He refused to discriminate against people because of their age, gender, race, religion, orientation, educational level, socio-economic status, or physical, mental, and emotional challenges; therefore, he was able to perform so many miracles, signs, and wonders.

Jesus loved the little children and allowed them to come to him regardless of their age (Matthew 19:13-15). Jesus loved the woman with the issue of blood and allowed her to touch him regardless of her gender (Mark 5:24-26). Jesus loved the woman at the well regardless of her Samaritan race and culture (John 4:1-24). Jesus loved Nicodemus regardless of his orthodox religious background (John 3:1-8). Jesus loved the woman caught in adultery regardless of her sexual behavior (John 8:1-11).

Jesus loved the widow who gave a penny regardless of her socio-economic status (Luke 21:1-3). Jesus loved the man at the pool of Bethesda regardless of his physical challenges (John 5:1-15). Jesus loved the young rich ruler regardless of his educational level (Luke 10:24-28). Jesus loved the man with the legion of demons regardless of his mental and emotional challenges (Mark 5:1-15).

As we follow Jesus' example to love all people regardless of how they are expressing, where they are, or what they have done, we will experience and perform more miracles, signs, and wonders.

_____

_____

_____

_____

_____

_____

_____

_____

_____

_____

_____

_____

_____

_____

ANGELS KEEP WATCH OVER ME

Bishop Juanita A. Gillis
Kingdom Covenant Ministries and Network
Baltimore, MD
COTEK, National Five-Fold Pastor

"For God shall give angels charge over you, to keep you in all your ways. They will bear you up with their hands, so that you do not injury your foot against a stone." Psalms 91:11-12, KSB

In 1989, I was living in Baltimore, but I was working in D.C. I took the train 99 percent of the time. On that day, we had a meeting at the church in Baltimore and I HAD to catch the train on time. I was running behind time and as I was running down the steps at the train station, I saw the train starting to pull away. The only thought that was running through my mind at the time was "I had to catch THIS train so that I was able to get to work on time, so I was able leave on time to get to the meeting at the church that evening."

The train was pulling off. I started running after the train and I thought, I will just throw myself onto the train. I saw it done on a commercial and it did not look hard. I then tried to throw myself on the train with a bag over my shoulder and pocketbook in my hand. I hit the train and I fell backwards. I fell into what felt like clouds and I felt myself being laid down on the ground, ever so gently.

The train stopped and the conductor ran back to me, angrily shouting to NEVER do that again and stated that there will always be another train coming. He then jumped onto the track to retrieve the shoe that fell on the track. I knew it was possible for me to have been on the track, not just my shoe. I realized that it was angels that caught me and gently laid me on the ground. I was in awe all day long and still am, even though that happened almost 35 years ago. I know it was Divine Protection that surrounded me so that I can accomplish the Divine Purpose that was planned for my life before I entered my mother's womb.

Angels are ever watching over us. They are keeping us in all our ways. We may never acknowledge them, but it does not stop them from fulfilling their purpose of protection. Do we allow people, places, or things to stop us from fulfilling our assignments? Let us be like the angels that work regardless. I try to acknowledge my angels when I am aware of their presence, the angels that I do not see but above all the angels that I do see.

Week 2 – Miracles of the Head and Face

Day 8 – All the way!
Day 9 – Give me back my ear!
Day 10 – It's about the glory!
Day 11 – Asked and Answered!
Day 12 – Let's Do it Again!
Day 13 – The Journey to Openness
Day 14 – It's About Time!

Day 8 – All the way!

Read – Mark 10:46-52

> *"Faith comes by hearing and hearing by the Word of God (Romans 10:17)."* KSB

One of the unique things about the healing of Bartimaeus is that we know his name. He was on a Jericho journey. Jericho means opportunity. As he moved along his journey, he gained opportunities. Although he was blind, he realized that sight was not his only sense. Bartimaeus used his sense of hearing, and he heard that Jesus performed healings. Let us use the senses that we have and allow them to guide us along the way. Instead of making excuses, move, even if we must do it with blindness.

On his Jericho journey, his path intersected with Jesus because Jesus was also on a journey. Jesus was on his journey of manifesting the Kingdom of God. They were divinely placed on their journeys, so they were going to meet. If we continue our path, it will intersect with everyone and everything necessary for our growth in consciousness. As paths cross, there will be miracles.

Bartimaeus heard Jesus and cried out, "Jesus, Son of David," which meant he recognized Jesus' lineage. Son of David means son of royalty. Bartimaeus means son of Timeaus, which means polluted and contaminated. When he joined his Timeaus with Jesus' David, he received the miracle of sight.

The only way to experience all the good that God has for us is to go all the way. Life is a journey, not a destination. The only way to see the end is to go all the way. Life is about experiences. The journey will yield lessons and blessings when we go all the way. Blindness was a part of Bartimaeus' journey. We all have had times when we were blinded by people, places, or things.

Describe a time in your life when you felt blindsided.

_____

_____

_____

_____

_____

_____

_____

_____

_____

_____

Day 9 – Give me back my ear!

Read – Luke 22:50-51

> *"Whoever has an ear to hear, let them hear (Matthew 11:15)."* KSB

The disciples felt anxious, worried, and scared because they knew Jesus was about to die. It is important to honor, respect, and feel our feelings. The heart becomes pure by acknowledging our feelings. Jesus was a feeling person. Feelings are not right or wrong. It is what we do with our feelings and how you channel the energy of our emotions.

As they were experiencing their feelings, they asked Jesus if they needed to fight to protect him. They tried to deal with an emotional challenge on a physical level instead of going deeper. Jesus told them, "No." They did not need to fight.

One of the disciples did not listen and reacted out of emotion. He did not balance his thoughts and feelings and reactively cut off the high priest's servant's ear. Just as fast as the man's ear was cut off, Jesus restored it. Jesus was a peacemaker and did not desire to die in anger. When Jesus attached the man's ear, it was fully restored and functioned properly. This miracle is the only time where hurt and healing happened in Jesus' presence.

The words, ear, hear, and heart, are similar. Our ears help us hear through the transitions of our hearts. Let us take time in the stillness and silence so we can hear what God is saying to us. Can you hear God? If not, experience God's healing power. Get your ear back!

Day 10 – It's about the glory!

Read – John 9:1-41

"I AM convinced that the sufferings of this present time are not worthy to be compared with the glory that will be revealed through us (Romans 8:18)." KSB

The healing of this blind man was unique, in that, he was born blind. It was unheard of that people who were born blind were able to receive their sight. With this miracle, Jesus made history by defying the odds and doing what seemed to be impossible. The miracle was really between Jesus, our Wayshower, and the young man. Because it was epic, so many people had questions, especially the disciples, the Pharisees, and the young man's parents.

The disciples questioned the cause of his blindness. They wondered whose sin caused the young man to be born blind. Jesus explained that it was not about sin but God being glorified. Many times, people associate sickness with sin and play the blame game. Let us become more like Jesus, our example, and focus on healing, health, and wholeness; instead of operating in a sin consciousness.

The Pharisees questioned the authenticity of the miracle, Jesus' sin status, and the observance of the Sabbath. Because they had never heard of a person being born blind being healed, they wondered if it was real. God can do the impossible and just because we have never seen, heard, or experienced something does not mean that God cannot do it.

The parents' questioned whether they were going to be excommunicated from the synagogue. Reluctantly, they confirmed that the miracle was authentic. They were more concerned about what people thought than praising God for their son's healing. The son was indeed exiled from his spiritual community because he publicly shared his testimony. His removal from the synagogue opened the door for him to have a relationship with God.

God received double glory because a man who was born blind was healed and developed a relationship with God. Every sickness is an opportunity for healing. Every healing is an opportunity for us to develop a deeper relationship with God.

Describe a painful experience in your life where God received the glory.

_____

_____

_____

_____

_____

_____

_____

_____

_____

_____

_____

Day 11 – Asked and Answered!

Read – Matthew 20:29-34

"Everyone who asks receives. Everyone who seeks finds. Everyone who knocks, it is opened to them (Matthew 7:8)." KSB

This healing account is unique because Jesus, our Wayshower, healed two blind men at the same time. The two men who were blind shouted out to Jesus for mercy. We do not know what caused them to become blind. But we do know that they asked for mercy to release and let go of what was keeping them blind. Mercy is when we do not receive the consequences that we do deserve. When we realize how merciful God is, we are not afraid to ask for our miracle.

The crowd tried to muffle the men who shouted. Instead of the men being muffled, they pumped up the volume and got louder. Do not let anyone muffle your praise. Do not let anyone stop you from doing what you feel is necessary to receive your miracle.

Because they refused to be muffled, they received a manifestation. The noise the blind men made produced an outcome that empowered them to see. When we pump up our Kingdom Practices, we also pump up the Kingdom Promises.

Both men received their sight at the same time. They had to be on one accord with their praise and they were on one accord with the performance of their miracle. They had to unify to bring healing at the same time. They received the manifestation together. They were co-conspirators for something good. The millennium of the 2000s has a partnership energy attached to it. This is the time for networking, supporting one another, and agreeing with one another for the highest and the best.

Day 12 – Let's Do It Again!

Read – Mark 8:22-26

"Remember from where you have fallen. Repent and repeat your first works so that when I come your candlestick will not be removed from its place (Revelation 2:5)." KSB

The miracle in our reading today is unique because it is a progressive healing. It shows us that sometimes miracles do not always happen immediately. It is no less a miracle because it happens over time or in the stages of the intervention, the improvement, and the ideal.

The first stage of his miracle was an intervention because people brought the man who was blind to Jesus Christ to heal him. When we are unable to get out of our own way, we need intervention. Be open to interventions from people who love you so that you can get to the next dimension of your healing. When Jesus met the man, he did another intervention. He touched him and led him by the hand. The man followed Jesus, a stranger, out of his comfort zone. Let the Lord intervene in your life by directing your path. Often our miracles are outside of our comfort zones.

Improvement was the second stage of this miracle. Once Jesus, who represents the Christ consciousness, got the man out of the familiar, he spat on his hands and mixed it with clay, and then put it on the man's blind eyes. Jesus was open for feedback and asked him what he saw. The man said he saw people walking as trees. His vision improved but was still distorted. He went from blind to blurry. God gives us improvements. Give God worship, thanksgiving, and praise for the improvements. The energy of celebration takes us to the next dimension of our healing.

Although grateful for improvement, Jesus did not settle for it. He repeated the process. He put the spit and clay on the man's eyes again. The second time, the man's vision was completely restored. The man's vision went from improved sight to ideal sight. He was able to see perfectly. The man saw clearly after Jesus repeated the process. We deserve the ideal, where everything functions according to God's purpose. When we settle for better, we do not receive God's best for us. Jesus, our Wayshower, showed us the power of doing things again. Let us keep repeating processes until we manifest all the good that God has for us.

Day 13 – The Journey to Openness

Read – Mark 7:31-37

> *"To the angel of the church in Philadelphia write: These are the words of him who is holy and true, who holds the key of David. What he opens no one can shut, and what he shuts no one can open (Revelation 3:7)."* KSB

We are born open, in fact, we enter the earth through an open womb. Then some drama or trauma happens in our lives that causes us to be closed. Something happens that we do not desire to see so we close our eyes. Something occurs that we do not want to hear so we close our ears. Something takes place and we do not want to feel additional pain, so we close our hearts. Something happens and we do not want to think about anymore, so we close our minds.

We did not start bitter, angry, or unforgiving. We become closed. The same way that we became closed, we can take a journey back to openness. Often, we go from being deadbolt locked, to locked, to closed, to cracked, to open. Jesus, our example, told the man, *"Ephphatha!"* which means be open. The Holy Spirit is telling us to be open so we can experience our miracle.

Often hearing challenges and speech challenges are connected. Jesus, our Wayshower, used unorthodox measures to heal this man who was both deaf and dumb. This man needed a miracle, and he was open and receptive to divine unlimited ideas to manifest it. Jesus, our example, took three unusual measures to heal the man: took him out of the town, put his finger in the man's ear, and spit on his tongue. Each action required a greater level of openness.

What are you willing to do to get your miracle?
_____
_____
_____
_____

What comfort are you willing to give up to receive your miracle?
_____
_____
_____
_____

God is able; are you willing and open to change?
_____
_____
_____
_____

Day 14 – It's About Time!

Read – John 4:46-54

"Humble yourselves; therefore, under the mighty hand of God and God will exalt you in due time (I Peter 5:6)." KSB

In the Greek language, there are two words for time. One is chronos. Chronos time has to do with seconds, minutes, hours, days, weeks, months, years, decades, centuries, and millenniums. We use chronos to set appointments and to schedule events. The other word for time is Kairos. Kairos means the right time or the perfect moment. We are unable to schedule Kairos time. It is a God thing.

Jesus healed the royal official's son without physical contact. This was the second occurrence in scripture where Jesus healed a person just by his words. The royal official was concerned about the time that his son was healed. When his servants told him the time, he realized that it was the exact time that Jesus spoke the words, "your son will live." In Kingdom, Kairos and chronos time come together as one. We call it the Kingdom Principle of Divine Timing. There is a divine timing in the universe, and everything happens exactly when it is supposed to happen.

In the text, there was a time for the son to be sick. There was a time for the father to meet Jesus. There was a time, 12 noon, for the son to be healed. There are no coincidences, and nothing happens by chance. We are not ahead of God, and we are not behind God. We are in tuned and lockstep with God's divine timing for our lives. It is our time for miracles, signs, and wonders.

THE FRUIT OF MY LIPS

Overseer Julius L. Ford
Kingdom Assembly of Grace and Truth, Inc., Spiritual Leader
Atlanta, GA
COTEK, General Secretary

"By him therefore let us offer the sacrifice of praise to God continually, that is, the fruit of our lips giving thanks to God's name. But to do good and do not forget to communicate: for with such sacrifices God is well pleased." Hebrews 13:15-16, KSB

January 2, 2001, is a day that marked my life with tragedy, trauma, terror, triumph, and testimony. Let us begin with the tragedy. As I traveled northbound on Charles Street approaching Friends School, I was in a head-on collision with a van while six additional vehicles sent my vehicle into a spin.

"Sir, you are okay. Give me your hand and listen carefully. Whatever you do, no matter what, do not remove your hand from your mouth until you see the doctor. Not even for the ambulance. This is very important." I remember hearing those words, I recall being fully awake throughout the reconstructive surgery of my mouth and neck. My face had hit the windshield during the collision, and shards of glass had nearly severed my upper lip and punctured my neck within centimeters of my jugular vein.

I know it sounds like the miracle of this story lends itself to the mastery of science. But I later learned that there was so much more. There were signs (supernatural manifestations) and wonders (divine interventions in nature). The first voice I heard while on the grounds of Friends School was a medical doctor that had witnessed the collision as he was leaving out of his house for work. He rushed over to take care of me until additional medical support arrived. This is proof of God's divine timing. The surgeon that reconstructed my lip and operated within centimeters of the major veins that transport blood from my heart to my brain was a visiting resident because no surgeons were readily available—God's divine provision at work.

When the forces of nature collided with the acts of God, my life was preserved. This incident was traumatic. Still, I was exactly where I was meant to be. I was divinely placed at the center of a major traffic collision to become part of something bigger. Living through the seven-vehicle collision was evidence of God's divine protection.

I chose to highlight this testimony with the excerpt from Hebrews 13 because I joined the Higher Dimensions Christian Center praise team while I was still ailing and visibly recovering from the collision. I came to Bible Study one evening and there was no one present to open the Wednesday Night service in song. So, I stood, alone, to render my testimony and a song of praise. That night, Bishop Dr. E. McDonald Wortham prophesied into my life that God was going to reward my sacrifice of praise with a full recovery. He concluded with the words, "I believe God!" He gave me a vile of anointing oil and instructed me to apply it to my wounds every day. Today, I offer the sacrifice of praise, continually…that is the fruit of my lips.

DIVINE INTERVENTION

Elder Katrina R. Johnson-Smith
Kingdom Covenant Ministries and Network
KRJS Ministries, Prayer Warrior
Baltimore, MD
COTEK, National Five-Fold Prophet
COTEK, School of Kingdom Prophets, Dean

As I reflect on my childhood, I cannot help but be overwhelmed by the profound sense of Divine Intervention that graced my life in those early years. At ten years old, my family and I found ourselves in a shelter in Harvey, Illinois, established by Catholic Charities. This sanctuary was a stark contrast to our previous living conditions, which lacked both physical and emotional support. For the first time, I truly felt sheltered.

I was always a loquacious child, full of enthusiasm and endless chatter. It was in this shelter that I crossed paths with Melissa*, a woman in search of safety/second chances. Melissa's children became my friends during their visits to the shelter and I was always excited to see them. Little did I know that three remarkable events were going to unfold that Christmas, revealing to me the profound depth of divine protection and love.

Melissa* asked my mother if I could deliver Christmas gifts to her children, which meant a bus ride into the city (Chicago). My mother, aware of the bond I shared with Melissa* and her children, agreed and I was on my way.

Melissa* and I arrived at an unfamiliar house, and it soon became evident that I was in a crack house. As chaos unfolded around me, I found myself young, alone, and in a toxic environment. Strangely, no one paid me any mind; it was as though I existed within an invisible bubble of protection.

I sat there for what felt like an eternity, yearning for escape. And then, a surge of courage enveloped me, prompting me to rise and run away from that place. There I was walking down the street, penniless, unaccompanied, and far from home. It was in this moment of vulnerability that divine intervention manifested itself.

A kind-hearted Caucasian man driving a brown Ford Thunderbird noticed me and pulled over. He asked me a few questions and, without hesitation, offered to take me home. Remarkably, I felt no fear. Instead, I felt a comforting presence. He took me to the gas station and bought me a bag of Vitner's BBQ potato chips and he drove me back to the shelter. I had NO idea that 24 hours had elapsed during my absence. The police were taking a missing person report from my worried mother when we arrived. I spoke with the authorities, assuring them that the kind man was no abductor but my hero.

The angel of the Lord encamped around me, shielded me from harm and, guided me to that compassionate stranger. Divine intervention remained a constant presence in my life. It reinforced my belief that God was my Source, and whenever I needed assistance, resources materialize miraculously. My journey as a child was marked by adversity, but it was also defined by the enduring grace of divine love and protection that continues to guide me to this day.

*Name changed to protect the individual's identity.

Week 3 – Diverse Miracles

Day 15 – This is how we do it!
Day 16 – You Give Me Fever!
Day 17 – Through the Roof!
Day 18 – How to Make the Swelling Go Down!
Day 19 – Healing Vocabulary
Day 20 – Testimony (Overseer Romell Parks-Weekly)
Day 21 – Testimony (Bishop Joshua L. Harris)

Day 15 – This is how we do it!

Read – Mark 3:1-5

"It is God working in you who gives you the will and the power to perform actions to bring God's good pleasure into manifestation (Philippians 2:13)." KSB

In today's reading, the text tells of a with a withered hand. Hands represent our ability to be productive. In scripture, the left represents the hand of work, and the right symbolizes the hand of favor. We do not know which hand was inoperable. We just know that the man with the withered hand was unable to work at his optimal level.

Like other Jews, Jesus, our example, went to the synagogue on the Sabbath. The tradition dictated that no work was to be done on the Sabbath. Jesus stretched beyond this tradition and performed this miracle for the man. When we stretch beyond limited beliefs, erroneous ideas, and faulty perceptions, we manifest miracles.

The Pharisees and other people in the synagogue had negative conversations about Jesus and waited for him to do something wrong. Both Jesus and the man with the withered hand stretched beyond the chatter. When we stretch beyond our own doubts and fears as well as the opinions and accusations of others, we are healed.

Through this miracle, Jesus, our Wayshower, showed us how to reach beyond our boxes and how to stretch into our miracle. The truth is that we are perfect, whole, and complete and when we are ready, we can stretch into this divine idea.

Day 16 – You Give Me Fever!

Read – Luke 4:38-39

"For the weapons that we fight with are not worldly. They are divine and mighty, empowering us to pull down strongholds (2 Corinthians 10:4)." KSB

When I was in Israel, I had the opportunity to visit the synagogue where Jesus, our Wayshower, worshipped. Less than a block from the synagogue was Peter's mother-in-law's house. People from all over the earth came to this house hoping to receive a miracle like she did.

In our reading for today, Jesus, who represents the Christ in us, came to Peter's mother-in-law's house and healed her of a fever. Houses represent states of consciousness. The more that we are aware of Christ in us, the greater our ability to heal ourselves from any sickness, pain, disease, discomfort, or dysfunction in our lives.

Fever is a symptom of a deeper issue. Fever is an indication that there is infection in the body. As our antibodies fight the infection, the fever breaks. It is important that we know the ways of being, seeing, thinking, speaking, and behaving that give us fever and cause us to be out of control. Our Kingdom principles help us fight infections. Our Kingdom practices empower us to establish healthy boundaries with people, places, and things.

_____

_____

_____

_____

Day 17 – Through the Roof!

Read – Luke 5:17-26

"The greatest demonstration of love is laying down your life for your friends (John 15:23)." KSB

Different from other people who were lame, the man in this story was not begging, alone, or feeling sorry for himself. He had friends. His friends desired him to see Jesus, our Wayshower, for healing and supported him in the process. Knowing that Jesus Christ was in the house, his friends went to the door. When they were unable to get in, they tried the window. When they were unsuccessful with the window, they went through the roof. True friends never give up on us and do not abandon us in our time of need.

His friends had faith and they demonstrated it through their works. Faith always finds a way when there appears to be no way. Our faith comes up with creative ideas to make the miracle happen. His friends were so determined for him to live a better life that they took the roof off the house. They opened their minds to the possibilities of what was able to happen once their friend met Jesus. They went through the layers of the roof and lowered the man to Jesus. Friends mirror us and help us work through the layers of stuff that stand in our way of healing, health, and wholeness.

When the man arrived in front of Jesus, Jesus said to him, "Your sins be forgiven." He does not address the man's issue directly. Instead, Jesus went directly to the root cause of his issue which was forgiveness. Often to receive our healing, we must receive forgiveness. Sickness is not because of sins but it manifests in our bodies because we refuse to receive and to give forgiveness. We all deserve grace and mercy. We know that we have accepted God's forgiveness when we forgive ourselves and forgive others.

The roof represents what is top of mind. The mind is the thinking part of the soul. It is our choice what we think about. We can get our thoughts from the mind of Christ, the highest state of consciousness, or from the limitations of our senses, or from the repetitive cycle of our past. The man who was lamed received his healing when he went deeper into his Christ consciousness. His healing journey is a powerful story of friendship, faith, and forgiveness.

Where are you in your love journey, wholeness path, and Kingdom voyage?

_____

_____

_____

How are you working through the layers to manifest your healing?

_____

_____

_____

How far will you go to support your friends?

_____

_____

_____

Day 18 – How to Make the Swelling Go Down!

Read – Luke 14:1-6

"Beloved, I desire above all things that you prosper and be in health even as your soul prospers (3 John 1:2)." KSB

In Jewish culture, eating with people meant that you agreed with their lifestyles. Meals were not casual; they were intentional. Even though Jesus, our Wayshower, was being watched, he ate with a prominent Pharisee whose name we do not know. Even though Jesus, our example, was being watched, he healed the swollen man. Even though Jesus, the pattern Son, was being watched, he performed the miracle on the Sabbath day.

Sometimes we are intimidated when we know that people are watching us. Jesus, the standard rule of measurement, shows us that we can be our authentic selves regardless of who's looking. Sometimes we feel afraid when people refuse to engage us in dialogue or answer our questions. Jesus, our elder brother, demonstrated for us that we can speak our truth independent of people's responses or lack thereof.

Swelling is an indication of infection or injury. Regardless of why the man was swollen, Jesus embraced him, healed him, and released him to go on with his life. Healing the man was more important than the opinions of the Pharisees or impending persecution for doing it on the Sabbath day when no work was to be done. When we prioritize, what is important to God and what we value regardless of what others think, we make the highest and best decisions.

_____

_____

_____

Day 19 – Healing Vocabulary

Read – Matthew 8:5-10

"Thanks be to God, who always causes us to triumph in Christ, and manifests through us in every place the sweet smell of godly knowledge (2 Corinthians 2:14)." KSB

In this story, Jesus had a conversation with a centurion, a high-ranking Roman soldier discussing his servant healing. Everyone who crosses our paths reflects a part of us. There is a part of us who is a centurion who understands our own power and authority. The centurion told Jesus that he did not need to go to his house to heal his servant; he just needed to "say the word." The centurion understood the power of words. Let us explore the words that the centurion spoke so that we can expand our healing vocabulary. Although the words: go, come, and do are simple, they have a lot of power.

The first vocabulary word is *go*. Sometimes, instead of telling things in our lives to go, we ask them to stay. Phrases like "it runs in my family," or "it has always been this way," invite sickness and pain to stay in our lives instead of going. Stop inviting disease and dysfunction to continue with you and your family. Stop creating a negative future based on past events.

Come is the second word on our vocabulary list. Invite the things that you desire to come into your life. Instead of sabotaging God's blessings with "you win some, you lose some" invite triumph to come into every facet of your life: health, relationships, and wealth. Let us expand our consciousness to the place where we win all the time, with everyone everywhere.

The third word that the centurion spoke to Jesus was *do*. There is a part that we play in our healing. Often, what we are praying about and taking medications for can be resolved through self-care actions such as changing our eating habits, drinking water, exercising, and getting our proper rest. Words do matter. Use your healing vocabulary to transform your life.

A SELF-CARE CHECK-IN AND CHALLENGE

How can you change your eating habits?
_____
_____
_____

How much water do you drink each day?
_____
_____
_____

How can you change your exercise regime to improve your overall health and wellness?
_____
_____
_____

It is suggested and scientifically proven that we function best with no less than 6-8 hours of uninterrupted sleep daily. How can you improve your time at rest?
_____
_____
_____

Day 20 – The Heritage to Heal and be a Healer

Overseer Romell Parks-Weekly
The Sanctuary, Spiritual Leader
St. Louis, MO
COTEK, National Five-fold Apostle
COTEK, Director of Executive Affairs

In the traditional church, divine healing was modeled as a roll of the dice. You would ask, beg, and plead with God to heal someone, and either He would, or He would not. We called it "faith," but we were just hoping… a'hopin' and a'prayin.'

As God began to open my eyes to the Kingdom back in 2016, one of the things God reformed in my thinking was my approach to healing. Rather than waiting to be begged to heal someone, God had given us the power and authority to heal. We simply had to exercise it. So, I began to follow in my own ministry the model set by Jesus, and the results followed.

One example of this took place after my church's (The Sanctuary) worship service one Sunday. As I was making my rounds greeting people, I came across someone who was sitting down, leaning over the back of the pew. Initially, I thought that she was sleeping, but I saw her moving her head from side to side, so I asked her if she was okay. Without looking up, she said that she had a migraine. If you know anything about migraines, they are not simple headaches. They often involve intense pain, nausea, and sensitivity to light and sound. The last thing you want is to be surrounded by people and noise while you are experiencing a migraine.

I asked the individual if she was open to me praying for her, and she said yes. I still call it "prayer" because that is a frame of reference that most people understand. I put my hand on her shoulder, and, without yelling, or jerking her head around as often done in the traditional charismatic/Pentecostal church that

I am accustomed to, I quietly spoke with confidence and authority and commanded the migraine to cease. I commanded the pain and throbbing to subside, for nausea to cease, and for her to be at peace. It took all of 15-20 seconds, after which I paused and waited another 15-20 seconds in silence.

After declaring her healing and giving it a moment to work, I asked her how she was feeling. She sat up and slowly began to open her eyes. As she blinked, a smile broke across her face as she declared that the migraine was quickly subsiding. A minute before, she was unable to open her eyes, but now, she was looking around and smiling, in awe of God's promise to be our Healer.

I find that the less I liturgize or ritualize ministering healing, and just make it a natural, normal part of my Kingdom citizenship, the better the results I see. It is my heritage to be healed, and to be a healer. I AM always grateful for opportunities to celebrate this manifestation of grace in the lives of others!

Day 21 – Impregnated with Purpose

Bishop Joshua L. Harris
JLH Ministries, Spiritual Leader, and CEO
Baltimore, MD
COTEK, Director of Special Affairs
COTEK, School of Kingdom Prophets, Provost

"Before I formed you in the womb, I knew you, before you were born, I set you apart; I appointed you as a prophet to the nations." Jeremiah 1:6, NIV

My mother was 42 years old when I was conceived. I believe, I was conceived on Valentine's Day. I was a special gift to my mother because my father forgot the box of chocolates!

She had two previous miscarriages and was told it was a very risky pregnancy. What the doctors did not know was my mother was impregnated with purpose. I had to be delivered and bring to fruition the conversation that God had with my purpose.

The doctors warned my mother that it was likely to have down syndrome and other cognitive challenges if she went full term. My mother looked unto Jesus, who was the author and finisher of her faith (Hebrews 12:2 KJV). God has allowed me to complete six-degree programs and currently working on my doctorate degree in organizational leadership. I do not feel tired.

I work as an assistant principal of Cathedral Christian Academy and at Coppin State University in library services. I am the global servant leader of Restoration Ministries and the Presiding Prelate of Restored and Renewed Covenant Churches.

Miracles, Signs, and Wonders!!! I AM a living miracle, sign, and wonder. God flows through me to perform miracles, signs, and wonders. There is nothing God cannot do, and you have not seen anything yet! Stay tuned.

Week 4 – Healing Lengthy Illnesses and Contagious Diseases

Day 22 – What kind of party are you having?
Day 23 – I Heal Myself!
Day 24 – Love Lifted Me!
Day 25 – What is going to take for you to Straighten Up?
Day 26 – From Healing to Wholeness
Day 27 – Testimony (Bishop Teto T. Saunders)
Day 28 – Testimony (Bishop Stacey S. Latimer)

Day 22 – What kind of party are you having?

Read – John 5:1-15

"Rejoice with those who rejoice and weep with those who weep (Romans 12:15)." KSB

Parties are an opportunity for people to come together and celebrate. Through parties, we celebrate the various life events such as birthdays, weddings, anniversaries, births, promotions, graduations, retirements, and so much more. The most basic party has good people, good food, and good music. Let us look at the miracle of the lame man being healed through the party lens: there were the pity party, the personal party, and the party poopers.

The pool party was an annual event that continued throughout the year. All kinds of people with various conditions came to the pool because once a year and an angel came to stir up the water. Whoever got in first was healed. People hung around the pool to get their miracle. Those who were not first had a pity party of disappointment, frustration, and complaining.

The man who had been lame for 38 years had a personal party with Jesus Christ. Jesus, our Wayshower, invited him to the healing party by asking him did he desire to be whole. At first, it was challenging for the man to respond to the invitation and to let go of the pity party of what was and what might have been. As his consciousness shifted to the present moment, he obeyed Jesus' instructions, to rise, take up his bed, and walk.

The Pharisees were party poopers. They were not happy for his healing because it was on the wrong day, the Sabbath, a day where carrying your bed was unacceptable. The healed man did not allow them to ruin his experience. The man celebrated that he was no longer the invalid that people called him. He was validated by God so he was no longer invalid. Everyone is not going to celebrate with us. Let us learn to celebrate ourselves with or without others.

Day 23 – I Heal Myself!

Read – Luke 8:43-48

> *"Now faith is the substance of things hoped for and the evidence of things not seen. By faith, the elders received a good report (Hebrews 11:1)."* KSB

We all have I.S.S.U.E.S. We all have Identified Situations Stretching Us Effectively. When we recognize our issues and work on them, we can heal ourselves. When we pretend that we do not have issues or define ourselves by them, we stay sick. We do not know the name of the woman with the issue of blood for 12 years. Through the process of treatments, touch, and a testimony she was able to heal herself and become whole.

Her Treatments
Women who were having their cycle were required by the law of Moses to be quarantined until the bleeding stopped. Nevertheless, the woman tried to heal herself by seeking multiple treatments. She went to various doctors and spent a lot of money, but her condition only grew worse. She did not just accept her diagnosis or prognosis. She was determined and used every treatment resource available to her to heal herself.

Her Touch
The woman who was weak and in pain heard the news that Jesus Christ was passing through town. She believed that there was so much healing power in his garment that if she touched his clothes she was going to be healed. All it took was a touch of faith and she stopped bleeding immediately.

Her Testimony
Hoping that no one noticed her, she tried to escape through the crowd, but Jesus, our Wayshower, felt the virtue leave his body and inquired about who touched him. He desired to know who she was and to hear her testimony.

After sharing her testimony, Jesus explained that he did not heal her, but she healed herself. Her faith not only healed her, but it made her whole. Like this woman, we have enough faith inside of us to heal ourselves and to become whole.

Modeling the healing process of the woman with the issue of blood, how can treatment, touch, and testimony bring about a miracle in your life?

_____
_____
_____
_____
_____
_____
_____
_____
_____
_____
_____
_____
_____

Day 24 – Love Lifted Me!

Read – Luke 5:12-14

"God has not given us the spirit of fear, but of power, love, and a sound mind (2 Timothy 1:7)." KSB

Leprosy comes from the Greek word lepra, which means scaly. People with leprosy were seen as unclean and treated as outcasts. In Jewish tradition, they saw lepers as smitten by God. For fear of contaminating others, lepers were only able to fellowship with lepers. The man took a risk by going to the synagogue to be with the people and Jesus, our Wayshower. His healing journey included being full, falling on his face, and finding his voice.

The man in today's reading was full of leprosy which normally indicates that he had the condition for a long time. Like the man, we are all full of something.

What are you full of?
Are you full of malice, envy, strife, hatred, greed, pride, jealousy, fear, dishonesty, anger, or judgment?

_____

_____

_____

_____

Are you full of love, joy, peace, faith, and goodness?

_____

_____

Do you have any addictions that are filling your life and stopping you from being fulfilled? Is your life full of purpose?

When the man approached Jesus Christ, he came to him with both humility and boldness. He showed his humility by falling on his face. When we are tired of suffering, we will fall prostrate in reverence to God. The man also made a bold public request, "Lord, make me clean." He found his voice and spoke loudly regardless of who was listening or paying attention.

Jesus, our example, touched the unclean and lonely man, and immediately his disease and disorder disappeared. Jesus, the miracle worker, defied the belief that the man was contagious and was able to infect him. He loved the man enough to touch him. This healing was visible to all in the synagogue and served as a testimony of God's love and power.

Day 25 – What is it going to take for you to Straighten Up?

Read – Luke 13:10-17

"Every valley will be filled, and every mountain and hill will be debased. The crooked will become straight, and the rough places will become smooth (Luke 3:5)." KSB

The woman in today's reading was bent over for 18 years. The back is one of the largest organs of the body and determines how many other organs function. Her back condition had an impact on her ability to walk, to work, and to enjoy her life. The Kingdom Principles empowered her to straighten up.

The Kingdom Principle of Divine Placement lets us know that we are exactly where we are supposed to be in every area of our lives. The woman was exactly where she was supposed to be to straighten up, the synagogue. The local assembly is the modern-day synagogue. We do not come to the house of prayer because we have it altogether, we come because there is always something in our lives that is crooked that can be straightened. Let us not judge ourselves or others for coming to the house of God with issues. It is the perfect place for resolution.

She was also in the right place to meet Jesus and to hear the word, "come forth." No matter where we have been. The Lord is always there to forgive us and give us another chance. No matter what we have done. There is always a Word from the Lord that gives us answers to our questions and solutions to our seeming problems.

Not only was the woman in the right place but she was there at the right time. She operated in Divine Timing. She was present in the synagogue on the Sabbath. The Sabbath, the seventh day of the week, was the day of worship for the Jews as a spiritual community. The number seven is a spiritual number which means completion. She learned all that she needed to learn through her bent over experience. It was now time for her to straighten up so that she was able to be all that she was destined to be.

What in your life is crooked?

_____

_____

_____

_____

What is it going to take for you to straighten up?

_____

_____

_____

_____

What is it going to take for you to become what God intended you to be?

_____

_____

_____

_____

Day 26 – From Healing to Wholeness

Read – Luke 12:11-19

"I pray God that your whole being: spirit, soul, and body be preserved and keep intact until Jesus returns (I Thessalonians 5:23)." KSB

Jesus was very active. In his travels to Jerusalem, he discovered ten men with leprosy. As stated in the law of Moses, they were commanded to be isolated so that they did not infect other people. Jesus heard their cries and simply told them to go show themselves to the priests. The priests were the only ones who were able to declare lepers clean thus allowing them to be reintegrated into society. With no evidence of physical change, the lepers operated in faith and obeyed Jesus' instructions. On their way to the priest, they noticed that their skin was clear, and they no longer had leprosy. As we move in the direction of our good, good manifests in our lives. God rewards our faith and our obedience with miracles.

One of the ten men, who was a Samaritan, went back to Jesus to express his gratitude. The Samaritan's thanksgiving moved him from healing to wholeness. Healing was the physical change in his body but wholeness was the complete restoration of every part of his life. Jesus was impressed with the man's faith and told him that his faith made him whole. No matter our condition, our faith can make us whole.

Jesus asked him about the other nine who did not return because they too had the same opportunity to be whole. Maximize the opportunities that are available to you regardless of what others do or do not do. The Samaritan man was one out of ten. He represented the tithe, the tenth. When we tithe our time, talents, and treasure from the energy of love and appreciation, we always set ourselves up to receive additional blessings.

Day 27 – Not Too Late for a Miracle

Bishop Teto T. Saunders
New Birth Fellowship Tabernacle Church, Spiritual Leader
Philadelphia, PA
COTEK, National Chaplain
COTEK, Dean of the Spiritual Leaders' Network

On January 14, 2022, my day started off with a terrible cough. I was scheduled to attend a Martin Luther King Jr. Memorial Service event and was not able to go. I self-medicated for about two weeks believing it was just a common cold. After two weeks, I finally got an appointment with my Primary Care Physician and got some prescribed medication. The medication did not immediately address the symptoms of the severe cough during the day and night sweats in the evening. I was not properly eating which brought about the onset of heartburn and constipation.

In the span of the next several weeks, I returned to the emergency room and had a follow-up visit with my primary care physician. Having undergone multiple assessments of my blood and chest, I was diagnosed with an uncommon disease called Sarcoidosis. This disease affects a number of organs.

Over the course of the next twelve months, I had follow-up visits with Pulmonologist, Ophthalmologist, Orthopedist monitoring the level of steroids which can cause damage to lungs, eyes, and bone structure.

I was told that I was going to be unable to perform daily tasks without precautions, be on steroids for life, and at some point, be unable to breath and speak. About three months into the treatment, I was in the edifice and there was a high praise that day. With the strength that I had, I laid down on the floor and praised God with my hands, and my healing process began immediately.

On June 2, 2023, I was taken completely off all medications. The frequency of my follow-ups decreased from weekly, to biweekly, to monthly, to quarterly. I was then discharged because God had worked a complete miracle in my body and the disease was considered dormant. There have been small flare-ups but nothing long term.

I arrived at convocation in July of 2023, with a severe cough and immediately contacted my Primary Care Physician and requested some Prednisone. I took an at-home COVID test, to be proactive. The cough immediately went away, letting me know my body may have been reacting to an occurrence of Sarcoidosis.

Upon my return to Philadelphia, we continued the small dosage of Prednisone and ordered chest x-rays, breathing test, and blood work. On September 20, 2023, the Pulmonary physician gave me the news that my lungs were all clear, and in fact are in better condition than they were twenty years ago. The physician requested to do some quarterly follow-ups but "I AM HEALED. I AM WHOLE. I AM A MIRACLE."

Day 28 – A Change of HAART

Bishop Stacey S. Latimer
Love Alive International Sanctuary of Praise, Spiritual Leader
Brooklyn, NY
COTEK, National Five-Fold Evangelist

As a national HIV/AIDS speaker, there are many people that know of my story; yet there is never a chance to tell it all at one time. The Lord has done so much, I just cannot tell it all. After being diagnosed with HIV in June of 1987, I was informed I had less than six months to live. There was no treatment, no cure, no medications at the time for HIV. There were some experimental treatments out there (AZT), but I was not led by the Lord to try it. I had no one to turn to but the Lord.

In 1994, protease inhibitors or the "cocktails" came on the scene as the new means of treating HIV and AIDS. Again, I was not interested, as they were still in the experimental stage. In 1996, a few of the drugs were showing great promise. The viral load test was now being used to measure the amount of virus in the blood stream. Treatment became more focused and targeted. My viral load measured well over one hundred thousand at that time. My doctor seemed very worried, and he conveyed those concerns to me. Out of fear of getting sick, along with the proven record of the few I knew using HAART, I began the new HARRT regiment. Two weeks in and everything seemed fine. At least I felt well.

During that time, I participated in doing volunteer work. It was a Wednesday. I was rushing trying to make sure I was not late to Bible Study. Earlier that afternoon after lunch, several people randomly began to ask if I felt, okay? I responded "yes," as I did. One or two people even asked me if, I was sure. I was so bothered by it that I went into the bathroom to check myself out and see if I was able to see what others were seeing. I looked okay to me. So, I kept going, and yes, people continued to ask me that question.

As I was driving home, I started to feel as though I was slightly dehydrated. I made it home. Drank some water and headed up the stairs toward my bedroom when I passed out on the stairs. When I came to, I called 911. The ambulance took me to the hospital. I was told the medication had permanently damaged my liver, and my gallbladder needed to come out. My eyes were jaundiced. I was very weak. They scheduled me to come back in two weeks to get my gallbladder removed.

Every day until I went back to the doctor, my Spiritual Leader had one of the leaders of the church come to my house, anoint me with oil, and pray for me. The Sunday before my appointment, I was picked up from home, brought to service, anointed with oil, and prayed for it and returned home. When I returned to the doctor on Tuesday, praise God, I was fully healed - liver and gallbladder.

Week 5 – Exorcisms & Resurrections

Day 29 – Casting out your demons!
Day 30 – Oink, Oink
Day 31 – Home Alone
Day 32 – Church devils
Day 33 – The Mighty I AM Power!
Day 34 – Essential Personnel Only!
Day 35 – Cancel the Contradiction!

Day 29 – Casting out your demons!

Read – Luke 8:1-4

"Mary Magdalene went to where the disciples were and told them that she had seen the LORD, and that he had spoken these things unto her (John 20:18)." KSB

Mary Magdalene was one of Jesus Christ's female disciples and a major supporter of his ministry. Part of her commitment to Jesus, our Wayshower, was that he exorcised her seven demons. We are not given the details of what her demons were or how her deliverance took place. We just know that her encounter with Jesus, our example, caused her to be free from what plagued her.

Demons represent lower states of consciousness. Demons symbolize our ego and that part of us that does not want to grow, change, unfold, and become who God has destined us to be. Demons are crystalized negativity that stands in the way of us healing and recovering from our lived experiences. We cast out our demons by releasing and letting go of feelings, perceptions, thoughts, words, and actions that are old, worn, obsolete, unproductive and do not serve us well.

There are seven common demons that most people must exorcise at some point in their lives to be successful. One demon is a poor self-image, believing that there is something wrong with us. We cast out this demon by affirming that we are perfect, whole, and complete. Low self-esteem, feeling that we are not good enough, is a demon that must be exorcised. We exorcise this demon by affirming that God made us good and called us very good. Another demon that we must cast out is lack of self-worth, feeling that we are unworthy because of our sins. We get free from this demon by remembering that as God's beloved offspring that we deserve all the good that life has to offer.

Guilt about what we have done wrong is a demon that must be constantly exorcised. We cast out guilt by accepting that we cannot change the past. The healthiest thing that we can do with our past is learn from it. Shame is a demon that causes us to lie and hide. It is the underlying belief that if people knew what we did that they will not love us. We are liberated from this demon by embracing God's unconditional, universal, perfect, and everlasting love.

Condemnation is a common demon that keeps us from experiencing our highest good. We cast it out when we stop judging ourselves and others. Affirm the truth that God is the only righteous judge; therefore, I do not judge anyone including myself. The seventh demon that must be exorcised is unforgiveness of God, ourselves, and others, God has forgiven me so I forgive myself and others.

_____

_____

_____

_____

Day 30 – Oink, Oink

Read – Mark 1:1-15

"For every creature of God is good. Nothing is to be refused if it received with thanksgiving because it is sanctified by the Word of God and prayer (I Timothy 4:4-5)." KSB

Jesus, our Wayshower, was not afraid of Satan, Lucifer, the devil, demons, or witchcraft. He realized that he had power over negativity no matter what form it manifested. Many people are afraid of demons and to eat pork because when Jesus Christ cast the legion of demons out of the Gerasene man, he commanded the demons to go into the pigs. A legion is a Roman term that refers to an army of 3000-6000. Following Jesus, our example, we too have authority over demons, and we have no need to fear demons or pork. We can live our lives free from fear and we can eat in moderation whatever we desire.

What some people call demonic possession is really the suppression of emotions. We often suppress our thoughts, feelings, opinions, and pasts. When we feel unimportant, we suppress ourselves. Instead of suppression, we can cast out our demons by expressing ourselves in safe spaces. Let us talk things out in counseling, with loyal friends, and close relatives instead of stuffing things. We must let it out to be free.

What some people label as demonic possession is really oppression of our expression of God. All of us are God's unique unrepeatable expressions of the Divine. Society oppresses many people due to their age, race, gender, religious beliefs, socio-economic status, educational level, orientation, family dynamic, credit history or criminal background. We cast out oppression by accessing the God and the good within us. The Kingdom Spiritual Practice of meditation, mindfulness, and breathing helps us to access the power and authority that is inside us all. When we know who we are, we stand up for our rights and society can no longer oppress us. Freedom is inside of us. When we know whose we are, we are free to tap into our God-given liberty.

What many people consider demonic possession is really people's failure to caress their own darkness. We all have light and darkness. We cast our demons when we caress both our light and darkness. Our light is our ability to love God, ourselves, and others. Our darkness is our stubborn refusal to change. Change takes place when we receive the lessons from our past experiences. Instead of hiding our past errors and pretending that we do not have darkness, let us caress it. Like we embrace the sun and the moon, let us embrace our own greater light and our lesser light so that we can be whole.

Day 31 – Home Alone

Read – Mark 7:24-30

"Beloved, I do not feel that I have arrived but this one thing I do, forgetting those things which are behind me, I press toward the mark for the prize of the high calling of God in Christ Jesus (Philippians 3:13)." KSB

In today's reading, a Greek woman left her demon-filled daughter home alone to go to Jesus Christ to seek deliverance for her daughter. Jesus, our Wayshower, was clear about his assignment and knew that his target audience was the Jews. Therefore, the woman and her daughter had to wait. The woman accepted Jesus' response willingly. She used the metaphor of a dog waiting for the scraps from the master's table. Impressed by her patience, Jesus, our example, told her to go home because her daughter was now free from her demons.

What many people consider demonic possession is really regression. When we are home alone for too long, we regress. We go back to our old ways of being, seeing, thinking, speaking, and behaving. We cast out regression with success. Let us go back to what we did when we felt successful. We do not have to regress; we can have success when we examine the things that worked for us and start doing those things again. We can create our own succession plan with success after success. We can move forward instead of going backward.

What many people call demonic possession is really an obsession. Being home alone for too long can cause the demon of obsession to manifest. Like the little girl in the text, we become obsessed with our "new" toys. We cast out the demon of obsession by finding our balance of time alone and time with others. Although people, places, and things may be good for us, too much of anyone or anything is not good. We do not have to obsess, we can press toward the mark of living a holistically healthy, balanced, and well-rounded life.

What some call demonic possession is really depression. Being home alone can bring out the demon of depression. Depression and gratitude cannot coexist. Spend time with family and friends that bring out the best in you. Do the things that bring you joy. We all feel depressed sometimes and need to increase our appreciation. Nevertheless, if the depression lasts for more than a week, seek the services of a mental health professional to support you in your healing journey.

List the things that you are thankful for in your life and document them in a journal.

_____
_____
_____
_____
_____
_____
_____
_____
_____
_____

Day 32 – Church devils

Read – Mark 1:21-28

"Come to me all who labor and are heavy laden and I will give you rest (Matthew 11:28)." KSB

One day while Jesus, our Wayshower, was in the synagogue teaching, a man came into the sanctuary who appeared to be possessed by the devil. Jesus Christ spoke to the demon with authority and told it to quietly leave. The demon followed the instructions of Jesus, our example, and came out of the man.

What many people call demonic possession is really a digression. We are all on a love journey. We are all on a wholeness path. We are all on a Kingdom voyage. When we digress from the direction of our purpose, we test our intentions and values. We can cast out the demon of digression through the Kingdom Practices of Vision and Visualization. When we have a clear vision of our destiny, we release distractions and stop digressing.

Some people that we think are possessed are really stressed. The way to cast out this devil of stress is to rest. Rest in the Lord and in the knowingness that ALL IS WELL. Stop trying to do things on your own. Life is not meant to be heavy, and ministry is not supposed to be hard. Allow the Holy Spirit to flow through you. Sometimes when our basic needs for food, water, sleep, recreation, and intimacy are not met, we can be irritable and short with people. Let us exorcise stress by taking care of ourselves and giving from the overflow of our saucers instead of the necessity of our cups.

The people in the synagogue were not only amazed at Jesus' wisdom to teach but at his power to exorcise demons. Like demons, things come up and out so that we can live a better life. Address your demons as they arise. Deal with issues as they occur. Let go of the erroneous idea that faith communities are utopias. Challenges can occur in any setting, and we have the power to handle whatever comes up whether it happens at home, community, school, work, or church.

_____

_____

_____

_____

_____

_____

_____

_____

_____

_____

_____

_____

_____

Day 33 – The Mighty I AM Power!

Read – John 11:21-43

"Jesus said to her, "I AM the resurrection and the life. The one who believes in me will live, even after they die (John 11:25)." KSB

Jesus, our Wayshower, loved his friend Lazarus who lived in Bethany. The threefold cord of Lazarus, Mary and Martha was Jesus' safe place. When Jesus, our example, heard that Lazarus was sick, he did not go to see him right away. He stayed back to deal with his emotions so when he did go, he was able to show up as the energy of the I AM. Let us deal with our emotions before we deal with the situation. Our emotions often get in the way of our miracles.

Two of the most powerful words that we can say are I AM. Not I can or I will, I AM. When we say I AM we are talking about the essence of our being which is divine. God is I AM that I AM, and we are I AM. Amid death, grief, and lost, Jesus affirmed, "I AM the resurrection and the life." Let us follow his example and use the mighty I AM power to create our lives. I AM is our authority and the power to manifest our desired outcomes.

Using the mighty I AM power, Jesus removed the stone. I AM gives us the power to remove anything that stands in the way of the good desires of our hearts. Using the mighty I AM power, Jesus also called Lazarus from the dead and Lazarus had to come forth. Death cannot stand in the way of the mighty I AM power. Using the mighty I AM power, Jesus commanded the grave clothes to let Lazarus go and they did. Even inanimate objects must respond to the mighty I AM power. We have the mighty I AM power, and we can perform miracles, signs, and wonders.

Day 34 – Essential Personnel Only!

Read – Mark 5:21-24

"Where two or three are gathered together in my name, there I AM in the midst of them (Matthew 18:20)." KSB

Raising Jarius' daughter from the dead was a progressive sign. When Jarius first came to Jesus, his daughter was gravely ill. While Jesus Christ performed the miracle for the woman with the issue of blood, the daughter's status changed from sickness to death. When Jesus, our Wayshower, arrived at the home of Jarius, a centurion ruler of the synagogue, there were people everywhere causing chaos. People represent states of consciousness. Jesus, our example, put everyone out of the house except for the essential personnel.

Jesus was essential personnel because he represented the Christ Consciousness unfolding in the experience. The Christ Consciousness is essential in demonstrating miracles, signs, and wonders. Having the Mind of Christ helps us to see the dead raised in our minds because it manifests in the physical realm.

The core disciples, Peter, James, and John were also essential personnel. Peter was essential because he represented faith. James was essential personnel because he symbolized wisdom. John was essential personnel because he represented love. Faith, wisdom, and love are required to perform miracles, signs, and wonders. Just as Peter, James, and John represented the words faith, wisdom, and love, you too, represent an attribute of God.

The young girl's parents were essential personnel. Jarius and his wife were necessary because it was their daughter and their house. When we invite Christ into the home of our hearts, we are giving God permission to move everyone and everything from the premises that are not mandatory for the fulfillment of our purpose.

What is your one word that you represent?

_____

_____

_____

_____

_____

Who are the essential personnel in your life?

_____

_____

_____

_____

_____

_____

THE MIRACLE OF HOPE

Overseer Samuel W. Hairston, IV
Better Living Kingdom Ministries, Spiritual Leader
Washington, DC
COTEK, Director of Local Assemblies

Most of my adolescent life was spent chasing the illusion of hope. I tried to be everything the church and society said I should be. I wanted to be a good boy, an honest son, a saved Christian and even a straight man. I never achieved any measure of those aspirations; instead, I found sexual abuse, rebellion, lies and addiction.

One thing that happened when I was young – I somehow slipped and fell from a three-story window and have lived to tell the story of that miracle. Another miracle came on October 16, 2008, God delivered me from a vicious addiction to crack cocaine and a few years later a lifelong addiction to sexual promiscuity. Successful therapy helped me understand how the two addictions were interconnected, but the application of Kingdom Principles has sustained me for over 14 years, and HOPE anchors my soul.

By the time I was 17 years old, I was preaching around the country and for the first time I met a female preacher who manifested signs, wonders, and miracles. Watching her teach, preach, and pray for people caused me to chase whatever it was she had. I wanted the power she possessed but was not willing to put in the time with prayer, study, fasting, and persecution.

Now that I have an authentic relationship with God, I no longer have a desire to chase after miracles; every day I wake up and look in the mirror I understand that I AM the miracle. I believe in the manifestation of the supernatural power of God, but I also know that I AM the earthen vessel through which God desires to manifest power (2 Corinthians 4:7).

Day 35 – Cancel the Contradiction!

Read – Luke 7:11-17

"All things work together for good for them who love God and who are the called according to God's purpose (Romans 8:28)." KSB

Nain means green pasture and fruitfulness. The widow of Nain's life was a contradiction to where she lived because her pastures were brown, and her life appeared to be empty. When she met Jesus Christ during her son's funeral procession, the contradictions in her life stopped.

The first contradiction was that she was a widow living in Nain. Her husband transitioned so her marriage was no longer green and fruitful. Through her encounter with Jesus, our Wayshower, she was able to make peace with her past. As a result of our relationship with God, we can let go disappointment from our past and keep the remains of the lessons and the blessings.

Another contraction in her life was burying her son. Parents never think about burying their offspring. They think of their offspring taking care of them when they are old, and they prepare to leave an inheritance for their children's children. Through the resurrection of her son, Jesus, who represents life, cancelled the funeral service and her contradiction as a parent.

Her son's resurrection gave her the confidence that all things are possible. The implications of this sign show us that no matter what we have lost, we too can have the hope of a better life of optimal health, harmonious relationships, and overflowing wealth. The life application of this sign illustrates that regardless of how bleak things appear a brighter future is always available.

MIRACLES

Dr. Lisamaya James
Living Well Ministries, Ministry Leader
Owings Mills, MD
COTEK, Director of Ecclesiastical Affairs

God has been so awesome to allow some miracles to come through my hands. I have the gift of healing that I discovered in my twenties. I experienced hot hands and need to lay hands on someone. I felt this tugging inside of me, pushing me towards people. I did not understand what was happening, though I trusted the process because I knew it was God. I went to someone and ask for permission to touch them. When they said yes, I proceeded. I took notice of the sensations in my hands. They got so hot, and then after a while, they cooled down. As I kept having this experience, when my hands were burning, healing took place. When my hands cooled down, it was done.

I love singing in choirs. The last choir I was in, they experienced the gift of healing through my hands. It was nothing for me to sing with a hand on a fellow choir member on either side of me, touching their sore shoulder or lower back. My hands were on fire, and it did not take long to cool down.

One day, one of my fellow choir members asked me to lay hands on her after rehearsal. I said, "yes." After choir rehearsal, she told me she thought she may have a broken rib. I laid my hands over the rib in the front and the back. As I did that, I closed my eyes, and God showed me the mending of the bone. My hands were on fire for a moment and then cooled down. I removed my hands, and I asked her to lift her arms. She did with no pain. We stood up, and she had no pain. We danced in celebration of what God had just done.

Week 6 – Signs and Wonders

Miracles, signs, and wonders are often used interchangeably. The major difference between a miracle and a sign is healing. A sign is a demonstration of God's power that does not have anything to do with sickness, pain, disease, discomfort, or dysfunction in the body. Jesus, our Wayshower, performed signs every time he took something that already existed and changed it to serve more people; like turning the water into wine. Another example of a sign is when he multiplied the two fish and five loaves of bread to feed thousands.

Jesus, our Wayshower, did miracles, signs, and wonders because he recognized his divinity. Different than miracles and signs, wonders have to do with nature. Some examples of Jesus Christ demonstrating his dominion over nature are defying gravity and walking on water as well as calming the raging sea with his words, "Peace be still."

Day 36 – Look What We Can Do!
Day 37 – Live Your Best Life!
Day 38 – Moving Mountains
Day 39 – The Great Awakening
Day 40 – One last fish sandwich
Day 41 – Show me the money
Day 42 – The Lifestyle of a Water Walker

Day 36 – Look What We Can Do!

Read – Matthew 14:13-21, 15:29-38

"He responded and said, it is written that people cannot live by bread alone, but by every word that proceeds from the mouth of God (Matthew 4:4)." KSB

In today's readings, the sign was large numbers of people being fed with very little food. In one scripture, Jesus, our Wayshower, fed four thousand men. In the other text, he fed five thousand men. Both scriptures, only count the men and not the women and the children. Therefore, he fed more people than the numbers reflect.

Both accounts have the same menu: fish and bread. However, in the feeding of the five thousand, he multiplied two fish and five loaves of bread. In the feeding of the four thousand, he multiplied a few fish and seven loaves of bread. In the feeding of the five thousand, he had twelve baskets of leftovers. In feeding of the four thousand, he had seven baskets of leftovers.

The feeding of the multitudes was not a sign that Jesus Christ performed alone; it was a joint effort that included the lad's lunch, the Lord's blessing, and the disciples' service. The lad was willing to share what he had with others. When we share what we have with others, God flows through us as vessels to perform miraculous signs. The way that Jesus, our example, performed the sign gives us a powerful ministry model. Like the fish and the bread, the Lord takes us, blesses us, breaks us, and distributes us as life-giving testimonies to others.

Jesus, our Wayshower, had thousands of followers but a small number of disciples, disciplined followers who left everything to follow him. The disciples brought the sign into manifestation by organizing the people, distributing the food, and gathering the baskets of leftovers. It was in the clean-up that they discovered they did not have just enough but more than enough. Today, we are lads with lunches, and we are the disciples through which miraculous signs happen. There is always a part for everyone to play. Discover your role and see what we can do together.

___

___

___

___

___

___

___

___

___

___

___

___

___

___

Day 37 – Live Your Best Life!

Read – John 2:1-11

"The thief comes to steal, kill, and destroy. I have come that you might have life and that more abundantly (John 10:10)." KSB

In our reading for today, we see Jesus Christ in a social setting. He attended a wedding and made a difference while he was there. Living our best lives means experiencing the goodness of God wherever we are and in whatever we are doing. Through the example of Jesus, our Wayshower, we move from existence to life, from life to abundant life, and from abundant life to life more abundantly which is our best life.

At the wedding in Cana, there was an appearance of lack. It was just an appearance. Mary, the mother of Jesus, dealt with the appearance of not having enough wine. Mary brought the appearance of wine sacristy to her son because she knew that he had the power to transform the situation. Do not deny the appearances of limitation; deal with them by bringing it to Jesus, who represents the Christ in us. We cannot live our best lives by hiding things that we do not like. We must address them from a higher consciousness.

Jesus gave instructions to the servers to get waterpots, fill them with water, and serve the contents to the people. The waterpots were normally used for ceremonial cleansing. To follow his instructions, they had to release their religious limitations and dogma. It was in their obedience of serving the people the water that they noticed the water had been turned into wine. For the water to turn to wine and produce a sign, you must follow divine instructions. Religion can put God in a box and can limit us. Let us release and let go of the limitations that stand in the way of receiving God's promises for us.

Are there appearances of limitation or lack in your life that you have ignored? How can you begin to address them in preparation for a miracle?

_____
_____
_____
_____
_____

What limiting religious belief stops you from living your best life?

_____
_____
_____
_____
_____
_____

FLOODED BY FAVOR

Bishop-designate Dr. Davina A. Jones
Today's Church, Assistant to the Spiritual Leader
Tampa Bay, FL
COTEK, Vice President of Five-Fold Affairs

Though they do not fit so neatly into the categories of miracles, signs, and wonders, several of these favored moments flooded my thoughts as I considered what testimony to share. I recognize many of them to be the work of grace (what I did not earn) and mercy (what I did not reap in totality). In keeping with this assignment and this theme, I have chosen to testify to a mental healing I experienced.

On October 8, 2010, the plan was for me and my significant other to drive from Jacksonville, Florida to Orlando, Florida to retrieve the rest of his belongings. While in Orlando, we were to have dinner with his three older children and his sister. We then planned to travel to Cocoa Beach, Florida to visit his mother. We had agreed to be married and live in Jacksonville. However, only one of us returned to Jacksonville. He was shot and killed in front of me and his children in Orlando, after an altercation he had with a young man he knew from his childhood.

In December of 2010, I was spending time with my family for Christmas. I knew that I was not feeling well, but it was not my leg, my arm, my eyes, my chest, or anything that I was able to describe physically. Thus, I did not know how to tell my family that I was not well.

One day when no one was at my mother's house except for me and my great niece that I was raising, a rush of anxiety and fear came from within me. I was deathly afraid. I felt like my brain was leaving my body. I was dying and I was not able to protect my four-year-old, who I often refer to as my niece-daughter. The only word I heard that made sense was "walk." I gently instructed the baby to put on shoes and that we were going for a walk. It was an unusually long walk for me, but short enough and hopefully slow enough to not abuse the child. We rested at a nearby restaurant, per her request. My mind comes back to me. I felt peace. We returned home as if nothing ever happened. With no medical treatment, my mind was immediately sustained. I initiated therapy a month later and stayed in treatment for two years. To God be the glory!

Day 38 – Moving Mountains

Read – Matthew 14:25-33 KSB

"For by your words you will be justified, and by your words you will be condemned (Matthew 12:37)." KSB

While Jesus Christ was on his way home from visiting Mary, Martha, and Lazarus, he saw a fig tree with beautiful leaves and no fruit. Jesus was hungry and was upset that the tree was not bearing fruit. Therefore, he cursed the tree and decreed that it was never going to produce fruit again.

Through this sign, Jesus, our Wayshower, shows that everything in life has a purpose. The fig tree's purpose was to bear fruit, and it was not fulfilling that purpose. Every person, place, and thing in our lives has a purpose. Let us look beyond the physical and discern the purpose behind everyone and everything in our lives.

The fig tree's purpose was to produce figs which were a source of nutrients, vitamins, and sustenance. Purpose empowers us to produce. Jesus was not content for the tree to take up space, having pretty leaves but not producing fruit. When we are aware of our purpose, we produce the good desires of our hearts and experience fulfillment.

The disciples were amazed by Jesus, our example, talking to the tree. He taught them the power of prayer through the Kingdom Practice of Scripture, Denials, and Affirmations. We, too, have the power to move mountains of sickness and drown them in the sea of optimal health. We have the power to move mountains of chaos and drown them in the sea of harmonious relationships. We have the power to move mountains of poverty and drown them in the sea of overflowing wealth.

Take inventory of the things in our lives and see if they produce according to their purpose.

_____

_____

_____

_____

_____

Research the highest mountain and the deepest sea and notice the difference in their dimensions.

_____

_____

_____

_____

_____

_____

Day 39 – The Great Awakening

Read – Matthew 8:23-27

"The peace of God which surpasses all understanding will keep your hearts and your minds through Christ Jesus (Philippians 4:7)." KSB

Storms come to test our strength and to educate us. Storms of life serve a purpose, and they are inevitable. As we grow in consciousness, we realize that challenges are for our good and empower us to trust God, learn, and grow forward. God always leads us through the storms and uses them for our benefit.

One of the major ways that Jesus Christ traveled was by boat. When he got in the boat, his disciples followed him. The cost of discipleship is giving up everything to follow Jesus, our Wayshower, everywhere. While on the boat, Jesus went to sleep, and a furious storm arose. The disciples woke him up and asked him to save them from drowning. Like Jesus sleeping on the boat, the Christ that is inside of us needs to be awakened. The storm in our lives is the perfect opportunity to wake up our sleeping Christ.

When Jesus, our example, awoke, he rebuked the winds and spoke peace. We have that same authority to speak to the storm in our lives and demand peace. After Jesus performed this wonder of stilling the wind and calming the waves, the disciples were in awe and asked, "What kind of man is this?"

_____

_____

_____

Day 40 – One last fish sandwich

Read – John 21:1-13

"He said to them, follow me and I will make you fishers of people (Matthew 4:19)." KSB

This passage shows the Alpha and Omega Concept. The alpha is the omega. How things begin is how they end. The disciples went back to fishing where they started when they first met Jesus Christ. He does not rebuke or chastise them. He has their backs even in their backsliding and backtracking. Jesus, our Wayshower, cooks for them even though they betrayed, denied, and forsook him. He cooked for them because he knew they needed one more fish sandwich. They required a post-resurrection experience.

As in the beginning of Jesus' ministry, the disciples again were fishing all night and catching nothing. We get frustrated with people when they repeatedly have the same issue. Some challenges resolve quickly, and others take more time. Remember God's grace, mercy, and patience with you and dealing with issues as opposed to being frustrated with others.

Jesus, our example, gave them new instructions on dealing with the old issue. Listen for the specificity of the new instructions. He invited them to fish from the right side, representing their divinity and favor instead of the left side, which is work. Let us operate from our right side instead of our left. It is important that we do things from the Spirit and not from our ego.

Because the disciples followed Jesus' instructions to fish from their right side, they received their increase. No matter how old the issue is, we experience an increase when we follow the new instruction. We receive huge miracles, signs, and wonders when we operate in our divinity and let go of human limitations. We receive large and super-sized fish. Jesus did not wait to cook the fish they caught. He already had fish to cook. Then, he also cooked the fish that they caught as a demonstration of abundance. This was their last fish sandwich, which meant that they had to catch, clean, and cook their own fish from this point forward.

_____

_____

_____

_____

_____

_____

_____

_____

_____

_____

_____

_____

_____

_____

Day 41 – Show me the money!

Read – Matthew 17:24-27

> *"The love of money is the root of all evil. Those who have coveted after it have left the faith and pierced themselves with many sorrows (I Timothy 6:10)."* KSB

Money is not evil; the love of money is evil. God desires each of us to live a prosperous, healthy, happy, and successful life. One of the Kingdom Promises is overflowing wealth. God gives us the power to achieve that wealth.

Everyone who was part of the Jewish temple had a temple tax. In addition to temple tax, they also had to pay their taxes to the Roman empire. Both Jesus, our Wayshower, and Peter, his disciples used the temple, so they had to pay their taxes. Jesus did not try to evade paying taxes; he paid what he owed.

Jesus, who represents the Christ consciousness, gave Peter a task to resolve the tax issue. He told Peter to go to the sea, hook a fish, and get the money out of the first fish's mouth. Often, we look for God to do things for us, but we are called to be in partnership with God. There are things that we need to do as well to demonstrate our faith. When he opened the fish's mouth, there was enough money to pay both of their taxes.

The money was already in the fish's mouth. All Peter had to do was exercise his faith by doing the tasks. Everything is already done in the invisible and intangible realm. Faith makes our good visible and tangible. The money is always there, and it is waiting for us to believe and receive it. Let us pray and operate in the Christ Consciousness knowing that it is already done.

Day 42 – The Lifestyle of a Water Walker

Read – Matthew 14:25-33

> *"If we say we abide in Christ Jesus, then we are to walk even as he walked (I John 2:6)."* KSB

Lifestyle is so much more than the external. Lifestyle is about our way of being, seeing, thinking, speaking, and behaving. The world is a lifestyle that leaves God out; the church is a lifestyle that has God in it, and Kingdom is a lifestyle where God is at the center. Peter started out as a comfortable boat sitter, then moved to be a ghostbuster and then onto a water walker. Like Peter, we can all evolve into water walkers.

The first thing that distinguished Peter from the other disciples is that he talked to what others saw as a ghost. Before we can be water walkers, we first have to be ghostbusters. We bust the ghost by talking to our fears, facing them head on, and walking towards them instead of running away from them.

Jesus Christ walked on water, and then Peter followed in his footsteps. If we keep following Jesus, our Wayshower, we will reach a point in consciousness where nothing is impossible, even walking on water. When we realize that we are in God and God is in us, we can go against the norm, statistics, history, and do things we have never been done previously. We can be trailblazers and trendsetters.

Peter walked on water for a while and then he started to sink when he lost his focus. When we take our focus off God, we begin to sink. Focusing on the situation, people, and past experiences causes us to sink. We can prevent ourselves from sinking when we focus on God and the possibilities.

When Peter started sinking, he asked Jesus Christ for help. If we start to sink while stepping out on faith and walking on water, let us follow Peter's example and ask for help. When Peter asked for help, Jesus stretched out his hand to pull him up.

God will always provide support for us when we ask. Sometimes we are so egotistical that we drown before we ask for help. Asking for help is a form of prayer.

Peter walked on water twice. The first time he did it by himself and walked to Jesus. Then he walked a second time with Jesus. The Lord is always our lifeline. Put yourself out there and walk on water repeatedly. Get out of the boat, walk on water, sink, ask for help and walk on water again. That is the lifestyle of a water walker.

_____

_____

_____

_____

_____

_____

_____

_____

_____

_____

SURVIVING SUICIDE

Deacon Renet Dennard Cole
Today's Church, Board President
Tampa Bay, FL
COTEK, National Mother
MOCI, Registrar

When I think of a miracle in my life, I immediately think of the evening I survived a suicide attempt. It was a quiet evening and my soon-to-be husband; James and I were returning from dinner. He and I were having a heated discussion regarding an incident at dinner. I had a few glasses of wine and so had he.

As our conversation grew stronger, he said he felt that it would be best for me to go to my parent's (Aunt and Uncle) house rather than my own or home with him. I immediately became upset, reached in the middle compartment, and grabbed the gun, loudly saying that I was not going anywhere. Obviously, I had given control of my thoughts to the wine. At that moment, I put the gun to my chest and pulled the trigger. He was stunned and I told him to pull over and let me out because I did not desire anyone, especially the police, to think that he had shot me. He refused, pulled over into a parking lot and called 911.

To this day have no idea what he said. All I know is that an ambulance came, but not the police. In that moment, I thought it was the end. At the time, I did not realize that because of God, I did not lose consciousness or blood. It was truly a miracle. I was admitted to the hospital but only stayed overnight. I was discharged the next day and when I spoke to the doctor, he said I could have easily been killed or seriously injured, but instead, I walked away with my life. He said that the bullet was lodged in a bone and that he and his colleague decided there was no reason to remove it. He also said that God had something for me to do and it was not up to me to decide my fate. Along with that, James decided to return the bullets and found out that they were defective.

Here I Am almost 50 years later living a holistically healthy, balanced, and well-rounded Kingdom life because of God's Divine Protection and Divine Timing. I thought then that since there was never a police report or a referral to a mental institution, I would never share this with anyone. Not realizing that this would be my testimony and I would share it with others who needed it for the rest of my life.

There are times when I go for x-rays and the technician will come out to me and say, "you have a bullet in your chest" and I will look shocked and say, "what!" That is always my signal to tell my story. Of course, there are other times as well, like right now.

The goodness, grace and mercy of God follows me, and I AM grateful. Because of Kingdom, I continuously learn and grow every day. The bullet is my reminder and being alive to share this testimony is my miracle.

Week 7 – These Works and Greater Works

Day 43 – More Time to Do Greater Works
Day 44 – Greater Works – More Housing
Day 45 – Greater Works – More Healing Places
Day 46 – Greater Works – More Freedom
Day 47 – Greater Works – More People
Day 48 – Greater Works – More Local Assemblies, Ministries and Businesses
Day 49 – Greater Works – More Writing

Day 43 – More Time to Do Greater Works

Read – John 5:19-37

"Truly, truly, I say to you, whoever believes in me will do the works that I do and even greater works than these because I must go to my Father (John 14:12)." KSB

Jesus Christ was a miracle, a sign, and a wonder and he performed miracles, signs, and wonders. Through Jesus' life and ministry so many of the ancient prophecies were fulfilled. He did greater works than the Old Testament prophets because his birth brought about an expansion in the consciousness of the Universe.

Jesus, our Wayshower, only lived on the earth physically for 33 years. His active ministry of preaching, teaching, healing, training his disciples, and leading the Kingdom Movement was only three and a half years. Therefore, he also told his disciples that they will do greater works than he did because his time was short.

After Jesus' ascension and the descent of the Holy Spirit, the consciousness of the Universe experienced another major expansion. Throughout the Books of Acts, we see the Holy Spirit flowing through the apostles to perform greater works. They had more time to do ministry and more people with whom to do it.

Today, we are the Body of Christ, and the consciousness of the Universe continues to expand with each generation. Everything that Jesus Christ was, we are. Everything that Jesus Christ said about himself, we can say about ourselves. Everything that Jesus Christ did, we can do and even greater works.

Day 44 – Greater Works – More Housing

Read – Matthew 24:31-46

"Jesus said to him, the foxes have holes. The birds of the air have nests, but the son of man has nowhere to lay his head (Matthew 8:20)." KSB

Anyone who does not have a lease or a mortgage in their name is considered homeless. Homelessness was a part of Jesus' experience. He traveled so much that he did not invest in having his own house. Jesus, our Wayshower, identified with homeless people. He said, when they housed the homeless that they were housing him.

The apostles did greater works by selling their property to ensure that everyone had what they needed. When people left everything, and moved to Jerusalem to be a part of the church, those who lived there shared what they had so that on one had to be homeless.

Today, we do greater works by housing the homeless in shelters and providing for their needs while they are displaced. In addition, we sponsor home buying programs and affordable housing grants. We also have laws that require developers to reserve a percentage of their living spaces for low-income families. Despite all that we do, homelessness continues to be a challenge in this country and abroad. Let us continue to find creative ways to meet the needs of all people.

_____

_____

_____

_____

Day 45 – Greater Works – More Healing Places

Read – Acts 5:11-16

"They brought the handkerchiefs and aprons that touched his body to those with diseases and they were healed and to those with evil spirits and they were cast out (Acts 19:12)." KSB

We are made in the image and likeness of God. God created our bodies to function in optimal health. Sickness, pain, and discomfort are not natural. Our natural state is healthy. That is why our bodies always attempt to heal themselves. Disease and dysfunction of any organ, system, or cell of our bodies is not normal. Our bodies' goal is homeostasis.

Jesus, our Wayshower, identified with people who were having health challenges. He said that whatever we do to others that we are doing to him. Although there is no biblical record of him being ill, he said that when his sheep visited the sick that they were visiting him.

The apostles, Jesus' disciples, did greater works than Jesus in the ways that they healed people and the number of people that they healed. Their shadows healed people and they used clothes to transfer healing energy.

Today, we do greater works through research and modern technology. We do greater works through traditional and plant-based medications. We do greater works through hospitals, nursing homes, rehabilitation centers and assisted living facilities. We do greater works through vaccines and outpatient procedures. Let us continue to take care of our bodies, lay hands on the sick, pray for healing, visit those who are having health challenges, support people who are recovering, invest in research for various cures, and study various healing modalities.

Day 46 – Greater Works – More Freedom

Read – Acts 16:19-40

"The Spirit of the Lord is in me and has anointed me to preach the gospel to the poor. God sent me to heal the brokenhearted, to preach deliverance to the captives, to empower the blind to recover their sight, and to liberate those who are abused (Luke 4:18)." KSB

Prison can be physical, mental, or emotional. Active addiction, being bound to a person, place, substance, or activity, can also be a form of prison. Jesus' ministry was about setting people free from anything that held them in bondage. The truth makes us free and empowers us to stay free.

Jesus, our Wayshower, identified with people who were in prison. He said that whatever we do to others that we are doing to him. Although he never physically went to prison, he said that when his sheep visited others that they were visiting him. We are all one. Whatever we do for others, we are doing for ourselves. The apostles, Jesus' disciples, did greater works than Jesus by being imprisoned, ministering to the people who were in prison, and miraculously being freed from prison.

Today, we do greater works through prison ministry. Not only do we visit people in prison, but we provide them with education and rehabilitation. We also sponsor re-entry into society and job placement programs. In addition to physical visitation, inmates can also do virtual visits with family and friends through phone calls and iPads. Let us continue to find creative ways to support anyone who is in prison or has been to prison.

Day 47 – Greater Works – More People

Read – Mark 16:13-20

"After you are filled with the Holy Ghost, you will have power and you will be my witnesses in Jerusalem, Judea, Samaria, and the uttermost parts of the earth (Acts 1:8)." KSB

Jesus, our Wayshower, loved people and preached to multitudes. A multitude is considered seventy or more people. After giving his audiences spiritual food, Jesus Christ fed natural food to five thousand men not including women and children. Including women and children, Jesus fed twenty to twenty-five thousand people and the consciousness of the Universe continues to expand so that we can reach more people.

Jesus' ministry was targeted to the Jews and those who were in Jerusalem, Judea, and Samaria. He prophesied that his disciples were going to reach people in the uttermost parts of the earth. He instructed them to go into all the world and preach the gospel to every creature. He commanded them to teach all nations and to make disciples of all people. They followed his instructions through by foot, animals, ship voyages and various missionary journeys.

Today, the consciousness of the Universe has expanded, and we travel to share the gospel by planes, trains, and automobiles. We do greater works through radio and television. We do greater works through conference calls, emails, text messages, and chat lines such as Clubhouse. We do greater works and gather as spiritual communities through streaming. We do greater works as electronic evangelists through various social media platforms such as Facebook, YouTube, Instagram, Twitter, TikTok, Snapchat, and the list goes on. Depending on our following, we can reach millions of people in minutes. Let us continue to be open and receptive to unlimited ideas that empower us to expand our reach with the Gospel of Jesus to the lost and the Gospel of the Kingdom to the church.

Day 48 – Greater Works – More Leaders, Assemblies, Ministries, and Businesses

Read – Matthew 16:13-20

"And we build upon the foundation of the apostles and prophets, with Jesus Christ himself being the chief corner stone (Ephesians 3:20)." KSB

There are many metaphors to describe the church. One is the body of Christ with Jesus being the head of the body. Another is a building. Jesus prophesied about the church and laid the foundation for the church. He promised to build it through his disciples.

Through the power of the Holy Spirit, Peter, an apostle of Jesus Christ to the Jews, established the church on the Day of Pentecost. Paul, an apostle of Jesus Christ to the Gentiles, expanded the church beyond Jerusalem and Antioch. Through Paul's missionary journeys, he established local assemblies in various cities and provinces.

We continue to do greater works by developing more leaders who pray, preach and practice Kingdom principles. We continue to do greater works by establishing local assemblies with physical and virtual members throughout the earth. We continue to do greater works by developing ministries, organizations, networks, fellowships, and alliances who meet the holistic and diverse needs of all people. We continue to do greater works by manifesting businesses that are Kingdom owned and operated.

Day 49 – Greater Works – More Writing

Read – John 8:1-11

"Write the things which you have seen, the things which are, and the things that will be (Revelation 1:19)." KSB

Jesus wrote on the ground when he was delivering the woman who was caught in adultery. There is no other biblical record of Jesus writing. In the synagogue, Jesus took the Old Testament writings and made them applicable to him and others. During his temptation in the wilderness, he kept referring to what was written.

Luke, a physician during the ministry of Jesus, did greater works by writing the most chapters in the New Testament. Paul, an apostle of Jesus Christ, did greater works by writing the most books in the New Testament. After Paul established a local assembly, he covered them through letters of encouragement and epistles of correction. Other writers like Peter, James, and John wrote general epistles and they were distributed among the local assemblies throughout various regions.

Today, we do greater works by using the most up-to-date information and technology for translating scriptures in every language that we know. We do greater works by not only having the handheld Bible, but we also have Bible applications available to download on our computers and phones. We do greater works by developing the Kingdom Study Bible that has Kingdom Perfection, Kingdom Process, Kingdom Principles, Kingdom Practices, and the Kingdom Promises in the commentary of the scripture with gender neutral language so that all people are included.

SEEING IS BELIEVING

Bishop Dr. Paulette M. Zimmerman
House of Prayer the In Gathering, Inc., Co-Founder
Greenville, SC
COTEK, Kingdom College of Bishops, Assistant Dean
COTEK, School of Kingdom Prophets, Faculty

One day I left the church at once following the service and I felt unusually tired, and I decided to take a brief nap. In my semi-sleeping state, I woke up and I was in the same area of the church where I had been for the service. However, instead of sitting in my seat, I was standing, and the church had burned to the ground, and I was looking up at the sky. I found myself sitting up in my bed and frightened by my dream. I was unable to decide if I was still dreaming, or wide awake and prepared to get up from my bed.

For the rest of the day, the vision that I had of the church in ruins stayed with me. I decided to share it with the pastor of the church. I called the pastor and shared my dream. I was disturbed by the fact that he was rude and curt, and accused me of being a troublemaker.

Several days passed, and the church administrator received a call from a pastor hosting a tent service and did not have sufficient insurance coverage. When the administrator attempted to add them as a rider to our insurance, she was informed that our policy had lapsed at least two to three weeks prior. In the dream, God was giving me a sign. The fire represented things being a blaze, and me being able to see the sky meant that the church was uncovered.

Today, I recognize that it was the beginning of my prophetic ability to "see" events before they happen, and to give warning signs to people preparing them for what was going to happen.

NARRATIVE WONDERS

Bishop Samuel L. Zimmerman
House of Prayer the In Gathering, Inc., Co-Founder
Greenville, SC
COTEK, Kingdom College of Bishops, Dean

In the fall several years ago, around Thanksgiving, in the middle of the night, I felt a compelling need to pray for a woman that I knew in passing at the Veteran's Administration clinic in St. Albans, NY. I sensed an urgency to pray and pray continuously, without an end time for the prayer. After the prayer moments, I decided to mention the sensation of urgency the next time I visited her at the VA Clinic.

A few months later I had an appointment at the Clinic and I stopped by the woman's station. She informed me that the same day that I prayed, her son had been shot several times during the robbery of a local convenience store. The young man was successfully treated and managed to talk with her. He told her that he was committed to serving God for the rest of his life. As a result of his miracle, he began consistently attending and serving in the church.

I do not know who else prayed for that young man and his mother that night, but I know that my assignment was to pray fervently and continuously for protection as well as healing. The prayer was a covering prayer for the household that suggested God's desire for Divine Provision and Protection. The Kingdom Practice of prayer included Quoting Scripture, Denials and Affirmations even though I was not aware of Kingdom Principles and Practices at that time. There was also time for Silence and Meditation during the time in devotion to focus on the presence of the Holy Spirit for that young man and his mother.

Unveiling of the Seal

Seal of the International Evangelist of COTEK

The Seal of the International Evangelist

At the top of the seal are **two herald horns**, paramount to the call on every believer's life to share the Gospel; first the of Jesus unto salvation (Romans 1:16) and second the Gospel of the Kingdom (Matthew 24:14). The shield, or crest is supported by the **Four Evangelists** of this great gospel; Matthew (the *angel*), Mark (the *lion*), Luke (the *ox*), and John (the *eagle*).

The **cross** represents the sacrifice of Jesus Christ (Mark 10:41-45) as our reminder that he is the propitiation for our sins (1 John 2:2) and the proclamation of our triumphant victory over sin (1 Corinthians 15:55-58). It is the Lord's life and legacy that give us liberty (John 8:36). Calvary remains at the center of evangelism.

The **shield** is divided into four quadrants, each depicting an element of the work of evangelism. The **lamp** is light in darkness, as well as a reminder to be prepared to shine, just as the wise virgins were, with our oil (anointing), wicks trimmed (pure motives and intentions) and burning (a living word of testimony) (Matthew 25:1-13).

Jesus declared, "I am the **door**: by me if any man enter in, he shall be saved, and shall go in and out, and find pasture (John 10:9-11)." The evangelist is charged to extend an invitation of light (Matthew 5:16) and love (John 3:16) that will bring lost souls to repentance, regeneration, and reconciliation.

Furthermore, Jesus fed his followers **F.I.S.H.** (Matthew 14:17-21), and equipped his disciples to become fishers that draw souls from the sea of humanity (Matthew 4:19). Fish are the universal symbol for evangelism in "The Way" (of Christianity).

Faithfully Inspiring Souls' Hope

Lastly, the great commission (Matthew 28:19) is the evangelist's commitment to Christian discipleship and human service. Our **hands** feed the hungry, give drink to the thirsty, clothe the naked, house those without shelter, and to visit those in need (Matthew 25:35-40).

The 12 Kingdom Practices for the Development of the Soul

1. **Reading, Studying, and Researching the Scriptures** – II Timothy 2:15
2. **Quoting Scriptures, Denials, and Affirmations** – Matthew 16:19
3. **Thanksgiving, Praise, and Worship** – John 4:24
4. **Fasting, Forgiving, and Feasting** – Isaiah 58:1-10
5. **Stillness, Movement, and Prayer Postures** – Psalm 46:10
6. **Silence, Sound, and Music** – Habakkuk 2:20
7. **Giving and Stewardship of Your Time, Talents and Treasure** – Galatians 6:6-10
8. **Fellowship with the Saints and Positive People, Mentoring and Networking** – Acts 2:41-47
9. **Visioning, Visualization, and Dreaming** – Habakkuk 2:1-4
10. **Meditation, Mindfulness, and Breathing** – Joshua 1:1-8
11. **Journaling, Writing and Publishing** – Revelation 1:19
12. **Witnessing, Sharing Your Testimony with Others, and Outreach** – Psalm 105:1

Kingdom Principles for Divine Living

THE KINGDOM PRINCIPLE OF DIVINE NATURE We believe the nature of God is love. We love God, ourselves, and everyone else. Who we are is Divine, created in the image and likeness of God (Matthew 22:34-40, John 10:30, Romans 8:38-39, Psalms 84:11).

THE KINGDOM PRINCIPLE OF DIVINE PURPOSE We believe that the general Divine purpose for all life is to conform to the image of the Christ consciousness. Every being is also born with a Divine specific purpose, our why, to be discovered and fulfilled (John 10:10, Romans 8:28-29, I Corinthians 12:3-14, Galatians 5:22-23, Ephesians 4:11- 16, Romans 14:17, Luke 17:20-21).

THE KINGDOM PRINCIPLE OF DIVINE ORDER There is a Divine Order in the universe, and everything that happens in this life is according to that Divine Order (Psalms 37:23, Galatians 6:6-10).

THE KINGDOM PRINCIPLE OF DIVINE TIMING There is a Divine Timing in the universe and that everything happens according to that Divine Timing (I Peter 5:6, Esther 4:14, Matthew 6:28-33).

THE KINGDOM PRINCIPLE OF DIVINE PLACEMENT There is a Divine Placement in the universe. We are precisely where we are supposed to be spiritually, mentally, emotionally, physically, geographically, financially, educationally, vocationally, relationally, and socially (Philippians 4:11, I Timothy 6:6).

THE KINGDOM PRINCIPLE OF DIVINE PROVISION God has already provided everything that we need naturally and spiritually. We believe that God is our Source of perfect health, wealth, and harmony in all relationships (II Peter 1:3- 4, Psalms 23, Psalms 37:4, Philippians 4:19, Luke 6:38).

THE KINGDOM PRINCIPLE OF DIVINE PROTECTION God divinely protects and encompasses us with a hedge of protection. Anything that gets through that hedge of protection to us was meant to be and intended for God's glory and our good (Psalms 34:7, Job 1:10, II Timothy 1:7, Isaiah 54:17, Hebrews 13:6, Psalms 27:1-2).